The Unity that Helps an
The Unity th

by John Woodhouse
published by Reform

John Woodhouse gave three talks on the theme of Unity at the Reform National Conference in 2001. This booklet is based on those talks.

Reform is a network of Anglican Evangelicals committed to continuous reformation of the church. We are committed to the reform of ourselves, our congregations and our world by the gospel.

Copies of this book are available from:
Reform, PO Box 1183, Sheffield S10 3YA
Telephone: 0114 230 9256
email: administrator@reform.org.uk

Contents

Introduction: Unity and division confused 4

I. **Unity: One God** 8

    1. The unity of God and the unity of Man
        One God and human unity
        Created to be "one"
        Unity and the Trinity
        Unity destroyed
        Unity promised
        Israel "assembled"
        One at last
      Human unity without God
        The unity of Babylon
      Unity in Adam
      Kinds of division
        Division by God's grace
        Division by man
        Division by God's judgment
        The promise
    2. Unity and the gospel of Jesus Christ
      The gospel proclaims unity
        The unity the gospel proclaims
      The gospel demands unity
        The unity the gospel demands
      The gospel divides
        The division the gospel creates
      The gospel that unites and divides
    3. The evangelical quest for "unity"
      Unity in agreement
      Unity despite disagreement
        Unity in experience

II. Unity: One Church 26

1. The "ecumenical" dream
   Ecumenical and evangelical "movements" in the 20th century
   Evangelicalism and the doctrine of the church
2. The gospel builds one church
   The church is the gathering God is gathering to himself
   This church is the end, not a means to an end
   A denomination is not a church
3. The church is "seen" in the gathering of believers
   The "visible" church and the "invisible" church
   When is a church a church?
   What, then, is the "Church of England"?
4. The unity of *this* church is to be "kept"
   The unity is not under threat
   The unity is under threat
   "Keep" the unity

III. Unity and Denominations 40

1. What is a denomination?
   A definition
   "Denominations" in the New Testament?
   Denominations in history
   The evangelical denominational dilemma
2. A denomination can express the unity of the Spirit
   Fellowship between congregations
   Freedom of conscience
   Cooperation
3. A denomination can oppose the unity of the Spirit
   Denominational centralism
   Denominational loyalty
   Denominational distinctiveness
4. The unity of the Spirit is both smaller and larger than the denomination
   The unity of the Spirit is unity in the gospel
   The unity of the Spirit divides the denomination
   The unity of the Spirit demands trans-denominational fellowship

Conclusion: The Unity that Helps and the Unity that Hinders .. 54

Introduction:
Unity and division confused

On the night before his death, our Lord Jesus Christ prayed:

> *"I am coming to you now, but I say these things while I am still in the world, so that they may have the full measure of my joy within them. I have given them your word and the world has hated them, for they are not of the world any more than I am of the world. My prayer is not that you take them out of the world but that you protect them from the evil one. They are not of the world, even as I am not of it. Sanctify them by the truth; your word is truth. As you sent me into the world, I have sent them into the world. For them I sanctify myself, that they too may be truly sanctified.*
>
> *"My prayer is not for them alone. I pray also for those who will believe in me through their message, that all of them may be one, Father, just as you are in me and I am in you. May they also be in us so that the world may believe that you have sent me. I have given them the glory that you gave me, that they may be one as we are one: I in them and you in me. May they be brought to complete unity to let the world know that you sent me and have loved them even as you have loved me." (John 17:13-23)*

Whenever the unity of Christians or between churches is discussed, Jesus' prayer "that all of them may be one" is likely to be cited. Although the context and therefore the proper meaning of these words is often disregarded, the importance of Jesus' prayer for unity must not be neglected. Among his last words before going to the cross was this extraordinary prayer that the unity of believers might be "just as" the unity in the Triune Godhead between the Father and the Son. "We behold in the mirror of His prayer, the Church exalted by faith to unity in God and union with God, and thus rendered capable of possessing the glory of the Son."[1]

The context of the prayer in the Gospel, following the upper room discourse and immediately before the passion narrative, indicates that the unity prayed for will be a consequence of his death, his "coming to" the Father (verse 13). The unity is of those who will believe in Jesus through the "word" of the apostles (verse 20). The anticipated outcome of this unity is "that the world may believe" that the Father has sent the Son (verse 21) and know that the Father has loved those who believe in Jesus as he has loved the Son (verse 23). The unity is established by the Son's indwelling of the believers and the Father's indwelling of the Son (verse 23). "What is this but the Divine unity reproduced on earth?"[2]

---

[1] F. Godet, *Commentary on the Gospel of St. John*, vol 3 (Edinburgh: T & T Clark, 1900), p. 214.
[2] Ibid., pp. 218-219.

But precisely what is this unity? What is its character? Where is it to be found? How is it manifested? What does it demand of us?

Clear and truthful thinking with regard to "unity" should focus our vision and shape our policies as we labour for the gospel in these days. Similarly, confused and mistaken ideas of unity are bound to lead to misdirected efforts.

Currently there is considerable confusion.

The confusion is evident in the way in which "divisiveness" has become a comprehensively negative category, applied absolutely to evaluate words, actions, policies and even persons. If a statement, a strategy, a proposal is judged to be "divisive," then it is unwelcome and likely to be rejected *for that reason*. For example, in my part of the world the Anglican Diocesan Synod has proposed that appropriate lay persons should be authorised to administer the Lord's Supper in church,[3] just as lay persons may be authorised to preach God's Word. The proposal is opposed by many Anglicans around the world for a variety of reasons. Some evangelicals oppose it for only one reason: it would be divisive. For some this is the only objection, but it is sufficient. *Because it would be divisive* (it is said) it ought not to be pursued (at this time).[4] Likewise many other proposals, statements and actions are rejected chiefly because of their potential to divide.

This is confused thinking, because it assumes that division is *always* to be avoided.

This confusion is probably influenced by today's culture of "tolerance." There is a tendency to welcome *whatever* unites and reject *whatever* divides. Unity is good. Division is bad. Perhaps some who are determined *not* to be shaped by the world take the opposite position and think that division is good and unity is bad! This, too, is confused thinking.

We need to understand that
- there is a unity that is godly (Jesus' prayed for it: "that they may be one as we are one" [Jn 17 11, 22]) and
- there is a unity that is ungodly ("Come, let us build ourselves a city, with a tower that reaches to the heavens, so that we may make a name for ourselves and not be scattered over the face of the whole earth." [Gen 11:4]).

There are policies, actions and words which promote and express the unity that pleases God.

---

[3] The word "administer" with reference to the Lord's Supper is preferred to the more common "preside." The former term is used in *The Book of Common Prayer* of 1662. The latter term has no precedent in the New Testament or Anglican formularies, and suggests a significance to the role that is not to be found in these documents. Hence it is preferable to speak of "lay administration," rather than "lay presidency," although both expressions refer to the same role.

[4] The issue and the views referred to are not new. The National Evangelical Congress at Nottingham in 1977 (NEAC 2) was warned by Michael Green that the authorisation of lay celebration would be unacceptable to anglo-catholics and therefore "divisive." J. Capon, *Evangelicals Tomorrow: A popular report of Nottingham 77, the National Evangelical Anglican Congress* (Glasgow: Collins, 1977), p. 79.

And there are policies, actions and words which advance a unity which God hates.

Likewise
- there is division which is godly (the one who prayed "that they may be one" also said "Do you think I came to bring peace on earth. No, I tell you, but division." [Lk 12:51]) and
- there is division which is ungodly ("watch out for those who cause divisions" [Rom 16:17]).

There are policies, actions and words which cause division and in the process honour God. There are policies, actions and words which cause division and thereby grieve the Holy Spirit of God (Eph 4:30-31).

I do not believe that we evangelicals are currently very good at distinguishing these things. We confuse them. And as Anglican evangelicals we have our own special Anglican confusions!

My aim in the following pages is to work at understanding and applying the scriptures in our present circumstances with respect to these confusions.

In the first part of this study, under the heading "Unity: One God," we will consider such questions as:
- What is the nature of the unity that matters to God?
- Where does it come from?
- How is it established?
- What kinds of actions, policies and words are consistent with that unity, and demanded by that unity?
- What kinds of actions, policies and words threaten it?

In this context we will reflect on the quest for unity among evangelicals.

Then, under the title "Unity: One Church," we will ask:
- How is unity related to church?
- Where is the *one* holy catholic and apostolic church?
- What is it?
- What is the nature of its unity?
- What kinds of actions, policies and words with regard to church are consistent with that unity, and demanded by that unity?
- What kinds of actions, policies and words threaten it?

Here we will consider some of the differences between the concerns of the ecumenical and evangelical movements.

Thirdly we will attempt to apply what we have learnt to particular problems facing evangelicals in the historic denominations: "Unity and denominations."

- What is a denomination?
- What is the nature of the unity (such as it is) shared by members of the Church of England, or, more complicated still, the so-called Anglican "comm-*union*"?
- Is this godly unity or ungodly unity?
- Are our divisions godly or ungodly?
- Anglican evangelicals are forced to address the question of the relationship between
    the unity they share with other evangelicals,
    the unity they share with evangelical Anglicans, and
    the unity they share with other Anglicans.
- What actions, policies and words should follow from our understanding of these matters?

We begin the concept of unity in fundamental terms: What is the importance of "one" in the Bible?

I.
Unity: One God

1. The Unity of God and the Unity of Man

In the Bible the significance of "one" and therefore the concept of "unity" begins with the fact that there is one God. The basis for the concept of unity is seen in the Bible's first sentence:

In the beginning God created the heavens and the earth. (Gen 1:1)

Since *one* God is the creator of all things, there is a *unity* to all things, a solidarity, an interconnectedness by virtue of the fact that all things are creatures of one God.

This biblical monotheism which is basic to the biblical idea of unity is expressed in the first commandment to God's people Israel:

You shall have no other gods before me. (Ex 20:3)

That so-called "practical monotheism" was based on an "in principle" monotheism:

"Hear, O Israel: The LORD our God, the LORD is one." (Dt 6:4)

"I am the LORD, and there is no other; apart from me there is no God." (Isa 45:5; cf. 46:9-10)

The implications of biblical monotheism are momentous. If there are many gods, or no god, it is difficult to see why one would expect to find unity in the world: why there should be any coherent relationship between things, between races, between people? There are convincing arguments that this is why modern science developed under the influence of biblical thought, but not elsewhere. The one God, creator and sustainer of all things, provides the basis for believing in and expecting consistency, inter-relatedness, unity in the world. There are similarly convincing reasons to think that postmodernism's scepticism about science and human knowledge is related to the decline in the influence of Biblical thought. Without the assumptions of biblical monotheism much that has been achieved under the influence of those assumptions may not be able to stand.

However the particular interest of the scriptures is the unity of humanity, based on the oneness of God.

One God and human unity

Biblical thinking about the character of human unity must begin where we have already begun: biblical monotheism and the doctrine of creation. The Bible presents the creation of humanity (Hebrew *adam*) as the pinnacle of God's creative work (Gen 1:26-27), and the object of his deliberate care (Gen 2:4-25).

Created to be "one"

We first encounter the idea of mankind's unity in the expansion of the concept of humanity created in (*or as*) God's image in Gen 1:27:

So God created man (adam) in his own image,
in the image of God he created him;
male and female he created them. (Gen 1:27; cf. 5:2)

The emphasis here is not directly on the *equality* of male and female (although there is an important sense in which that is implied). What we have here is the notion of *unity*. In the parallelism of the Hebrew poetry the plurality of male and female ("them") is a unity ("him"). Genesis 1 presents the *unity* of male and female.

In Genesis 2 this is expressed in the unity of the marriage bond:

For this reason a man will leave his father and mother and be united to his wife, and they will become one flesh. (Gen 2:24)

The *two* "become *one* flesh," a unity.

It is important for us to observe that the unity does not consist simply in sameness or equality. There is sameness ("bone of my bones and flesh of my flesh" [Gen 2:23]), but there is also distinction. In their *oppositeness*, as male and female, they are "one." The unity is itself created, given in the creation, by the will of the creator. The Bible does not explain the "oneness" simply in terms of shared characteristics, or the like, but the oneness is presented as the outcome of God's creative act. The "them" of Gen 1:27 is a "him", the two of Gen 2:24 become "one," by God's will and action.

Unity and the Trinity

Some have even suggested that the creation of this plural unity is a reflection of the Trinity. It is noted that when God speaks in Gen 1:26, he does so in the plural:

*Then God said, "Let **us** make man in **our** image, in **our** likeness ...* (Gen 1:26)

The image and likeness of the God who speaks in this grammatical plural turns out to be a being in relationship: *adam* as male and female.

Whether or not it is reasonable to see a reflection of the unity of the persons of the triune Godhead in the unity of *adam* in the wording of Genesis 1 is a matter of debate. There are other plausible explanations of the plurals of Gen 1:26.

However the New Testament certainly draws inferences from the inner relations of the Trinity to human relationships. In particular we have already noted that the unity of believers for which

Jesus prayed is "just as" the Father and the Son are one (John 17:21).[5] In the light of the whole biblical revelation, it is therefore appropriate to see the intended unity of humanity from the beginning in relation to the unity of the Father and the Son and the Holy Spirit.

Unity destroyed

The rift between the Creator and his creatures caused by the disobedience of *adam* (Gen 3) resulted in his expulsion from the Garden of Eden, and the corruption of human life. In particular the foundational Biblical history (Gen 3-11) displays the shattering of the unity of humanity. After the Fall, man *accuses* woman (Gen 3:12). Brother is *angry* with brother and *murders* him (Gen 4:5b, 8). Indeed the earth became "corrupt in God's sight and full of *violence*" (Gen 6:11). Finally, the Lord "confused the language of the whole world" and "scattered them over the face of the earth" (Gen 11:9), leaving the human race in a condition of profound disunity.

The situation described in Gen 11:9 is the essential state of the world today. Unity appears impossible. The barriers between nations and peoples seem insurmountable.

Unity promised

However the sequel to the tragic story of humanity in Gen 3-11 is the new word that God spoke to a man named Abram (re-named Abraham in Gen 17:5):

> *"Leave your country, your people and your father's household and go to the land I will show you.*
>
> *"I will make you into a great nation*
> *and I will bless you;*
>
> *I will make your name great,*
> *and you will be a blessing.*
>
> *I will bless those who bless you,*
> *and whoever curses you I will curse;*
>
> *and all peoples on earth will*
> *be blessed through you."* (Gen 12:1-3)

The importance of this promise for the message of the whole Bible cannot be overstated. The apostle Paul will call it "the gospel preached in advance" (Gal 3:8). The fulfilment of this promise will lead to the apostle's great affirmation of unity:

> *There is neither Jew nor Greek, slave nor free, male nor female, for you are all one in Christ Jesus.* (Gal 3:28)

This outcome is implicit in the promise. From Abram there will be one "great nation." Through Abraham all the families of the earth will be blessed. All will be united in the one source of blessing.

---

[5] Cf. 1Cor 11:3 in context.

The whole Bible story, from Genesis 12 onwards, is the account of God's faithfulness to this promise he made to Abraham.

Israel "assembled"

The Old Testament history of Israel is a substantial part of that account. As we follow that story we see something of the realisation of the promise to Abraham, and therefore something of the re-establishment of unity.

When the people of Israel assembled at Mount Sinai after the exodus, God said to them:

> *"You yourselves have seen what I did to Egypt, and how I carried you on eagles' wings and brought you to myself."* (Ex 19:4)

Here was Israel, one nation, together before the Lord. Moses later recalled God's instruction on that day:

> *"Assemble the people before me to hear my words so that they may learn to revere me as long as they live in the land and may teach them to their children."* (Dt 4:10)

The day became remembered as "the day of the assembly," the day of the gathering together (Dt 9:10; 10:4). The Hebrew word for "assembly" is *qahal*; the Greek equivalent is *ekklesia*, often translated "church" in the New Testament.

Centuries later, in the days of Solomon, when the temple on Mount Zion was completed, we see another scene in which the people of Israel appear as one great assembly:

> *So Solomon observed the festival at that time, and all Israel with him — a vast assembly, people from Lebo Hamath to the Wadi of Egypt.* (1Kgs 8:65a)

One at last

If we pass from the accounts of Old Testament Israel's experience to the Bible's presentation of the end, the goal of all history, we see that these scenes of Israel's history will finally be surpassed by an assembly of unimaginable proportions. John was given a vision of that final assembly:

> *After this I looked and there before me was a great multitude that no one could count, from every nation, tribe, people and language, standing before the throne and in front of the Lamb. They were wearing white robes and were holding palm branches in their hands. And they cried out in a loud voice:*
>
> > *"Salvation belongs to our God,*
> >
> > *who sits on the throne,*
> >
> > *and to the Lamb."*
> >
> > ...
> >
> > *"For the Lamb at the centre of the throne will be their shepherd;*

> *he will lead them to springs of living water.*
> *And God will wipe away every tear from their eyes."* (Rev 7:9-10, 17)

One great multitude, before the one throne, with one shepherd, with one voice praises "our God" and "the Lamb."

We have passed over the essential events that account for the movement from Israel's Old Testament assembly to the ultimate assembly gathered from every nation. This omission will be addressed shortly. The point at this stage, however, is that our understanding of unity must be shaped by the broad biblical context: the unity of God and the consequent unity of mankind which is his will, and which he will finally establish. The Bible's message, of course, is centrally about what God, in his wisdom, grace and power has done to accomplish this. To this story we will return.

Human unity without God

We need to be aware that the Biblical ideal of human unity stands against alternative understandings, of which there are many. A concept of unity (less potent, I would suggest, than that based on biblical monotheism) has had a place in various philosophical systems. It is as though the creator's ideal of unity for the human race has forced itself on thinkers who have sought to explain or understand it in various ways. The Greeks and the Romans developed various concepts of the unity of humanity. There were arguments about whether there was a common human nature, and if so what constituted it. There was a view that human unity was effected by the bonds of society, particularly of law. The Romans had an idea of a world community, united militarily under Rome. There was considerable thought and argument related to such concepts of unity in New Testament times.[6] Likewise various competing understandings of human unity persist today.

In the Bible, alongside the story of the unity God wills for mankind and which he will bring to pass, there is the story of an alternative kind of unity. Humanity, which has shattered the unity under God for which it was created, nevertheless seeks to overcome its disunity.

The unity of Babylon

The Bible's presentation of the foundational human history concludes with an account of the attempt by a united human race to establish its greatness, security and unity by the building of a city (Gen 11:1-9).

The account begins:

> *Now the whole earth had one language and the same words.* (Gen 11:1 NRSV)

We can only imagine what humanity could be if there were no language "barriers" (as we call them). The people of Genesis 11 used their common language to formulate a co-operative project.

---

[6] W.F. Taylor, "Unity, Unity of Humanity," *The Anchor Bible Dictionary* (New York: Doubleday, 1992) 6:746-749.

What a project it was! It was a scheme to build a united human community, one society, by united achievement, by shared greatness, by mutual protection:

> *"Come, let us build ourselves a city, with a tower that reaches to the heavens, so that we may make a name for ourselves and not be scattered over the face of the whole earth."* (Gen 11:4)

Here is the scheme to establish human unity, without God. This would be a society centred on itself—its self achievements, its self aggrandisement, its self fulfilment, its self satisfaction. This is the unity of Babylon.

However, Genesis 11 tells us that God would not allow such a unity to succeed. He confused the language and scattered the people over the face of the whole earth. God's judgment came in the form of shattering the unity of godless humanity (Gen 11:9). Attempts to establish such a unity have been frustrated ever since.

Unity in Adam

There is another sense in which the human race since the Fall experiences unity. Paul presents the unity of mankind "in Adam." This is a profoundly negative state of affairs.

It is unity in sin:

> *... just as sin entered the world through one man, ... [and] all sinned.* (Rom 5:12)
>
> *... through the disobedience of the one man the many were made sinners ...* (Rom 5:19)

Therefore humanity is united in being under condemnation:

> *The judgment followed one sin and brought condemnation ...* (Rom 5:16)
>
> *... the result of one trespass was condemnation for all men ...* (Rom 5:18)
>
> *The wrath of God is being revealed from heaven against all the godlessness and wickedness of men.* (Rom 1:18)

Consequently, humanity is united in death:

> *... in Adam all die ...* (1Cor 15:22)
>
> *... the many died by the trespass of the one man ...* (Rom 5:15)
>
> *... by the trespass of the one man, death reigned through that one man ...* (Rom 5:17)

The usual distinctions in humanity do not break this unity:

> *... Jews and Gentiles alike are all under sin.* (Rom 3:9)
>
> *There is no difference [between Jew and Greek], for all have sinned and fall short of the glory of God.* (Rom 3:22b-23)

Broadly speaking we have seen three kinds of human unity:

(1) The unity intended by God, and promised by him. We will see that this unity is that for which Jesus prayed (John 17:11, 20-23).

(2) The unity sought by human beings in defiance of God, but which God has made unattainable. This may have all the impressiveness of the Babylonian city with its tower.

(3) The unity in sin, condemnation and death. This is the actual state of humanity without God.

Confusion arises, as we will see, when we fail to distinguish examples of (2) from the reality of (1).

Kinds of division

It is equally important to recognise that there are various kinds of disunity or division within humanity which must be understood differently. We may note at least three kinds of division corresponding to the three kinds of unity.

Division by God's grace

First, there is the division established by God himself as an act of his grace.

The Old Testament emphasises God's *separation* of Israel from the nations. God separated Israel from the nations in order that it might be "a kingdom of priests and a holy nation" (Ex 19:6). This defining expression indicates the separateness of Israel from the other nations. Ultimately this will be for the benefit of the nations ("for the whole earth is mine" [Ex 19:5b]). God's purpose to bless all the families of the earth through Israel (Gen 12:3) involved an essential separation of Israel from the nations. The Leviticus command that Israel must be "holy" is essentially a command to be separate (cf. Lev 15:31). Once humanity had rejected God, redemption involved choosing a people who would be separate from the rest of humanity.

God still makes this fundamental division between his people and the world (see 2Cor 6:17; 1Pet 2:11-12; Rev 18:4).

Division by man

A second kind of division is quite different. Human sin, which from one point of view unites all people "in Adam," also sets them against one another. We have already observed this in Genesis 3-11. Accusation, anger, murder and violence characterise human relationships since the Fall.

One important feature of the Law given by God to Israel at Mount Sinai was to protect the unity of the newly established nation. Children must honour their parents. One must not murder another, or commit adultery against another, or steal from another, or give false testimony against another, or covet what belongs to another. The people that lived in obedience to this Law, faithful to the God who had brought them to himself, would be a united community.

However, Israel failed. In due course the prophets brought their message condemning Israel's disobedience. Israel's failure shattered the nation's unity. Perhaps this is most vividly illustrated in the message of the prophet Amos to the northern kingdom in the 8th century BC:

> *This is what the LORD says:*
>
> *"For three sins of Israel,*
> *even for four, I will not turn back [my wrath].*
>
> *They sell the righteous for silver,*
> *and the needy for a pair of sandals.*
>
> *They trample on the heads of the poor*
> *as upon the dust of the ground*
> *and deny justice to the oppressed."* (Am 2:6-7a)

Israel had become like the other nations, and community life was marked by violence and oppression. Human sin is divisive. Both the history of Israel and the history of humanity display this fact.

Division by God's judgment

There is a third perspective on human disunity. God has a hand in the division of humanity, too. The attempts to construct a unity without God are frustrated by God himself. One of the forms of God's judgment according to the Old Testament record has been "scattering."

We have already seen this with regard to the early human race at Babel (Gen 11:1-9).

> *That is why it was called Babel — because there the LORD confused the language of the whole world. From there the LORD **scattered** them over the face of the whole earth.* (Gen 11:9)

When Israel followed the same path of arrogant defiance of God, the same consequence followed. The warning had been given as early as Mount Sinai:

> *"If in spite of this you still do not listen to me but continue to be hostile toward me, ... I will **scatter** you among the nations and will draw out my sword and pursue you. Your land will be laid waste, and your cities will lie in ruins."* (Lev 26:27, 33)

It was reiterated by the prophets:

> *The LORD said, "It is because they have forsaken my law, which I set before them; they have not obeyed me or followed my law. Instead, they have followed the stubbornness of their hearts; they have followed the Baals, as their fathers taught them." Therefore, this is what the LORD Almighty, the God of Israel, says: "See, I will make this people eat bitter food and drink poisoned water. I will **scatter** them among nations that neither they nor their fathers have known, and I will pursue them with the sword until I have destroyed them."* (Jer 9:13-16)

> *"They will know that I am the LORD, when I **disperse** them among the nations and **scatter** them through the countries."* (Ezek 12:15)

This judgment came, especially in the conquest of the northern kingdom of Israel by the Assyrians in 722 BC and of the southern kingdom of Judah by the Babylonians in 587 BC. God's judgment on Israel, as on humanity at Babel, took the form of the destruction of their unity. They were scattered.

Our understanding of human unity must involve recognising at least these three different kinds of division between human beings:

(1) The division which God, in his grace, has established between his people and the world, for the sake of the world: "in the world, but not of the world."

(2) The division caused by human sin. Defiance of God does not produce the unity that may be sought in Babylon. Babylon is a deeply divided community.

(3) The division which is God's judgment. This is the divine dimension to the consequences of human sin. God himself frustrates human attempts to unite in defiance of God.

Part of the contemporary confusion, as we will see, arises from a failure to distinguish (1) from (2).

The promise

When God's judgement fell on Israel, and the nation was "scattered," there was a promise that out of his compassion God would again gather his people. The failure of Israel did not erase the faithfulness of God to his promise to Abraham.

> *When all these blessings and curses I have set before you come upon you and you take them to heart wherever the LORD your God disperses you among the nations, and when you and your children return to the LORD your God and obey him with all your heart and with all your soul according to everything I command you today, then the LORD your God will restore your fortunes and have compassion on you and* **gather** *you again from all the nations where he scattered you. Even if you have been banished to the most distant land under the heavens, from there the LORD your God will* **gather** *you and bring you back.* (Deut 30:1-4)

This promise became a theme of the Old Testament prophets:

> *He will raise a banner for the nations and* **gather** *the exiles of Israel; he will assemble the scattered people of Judah from the four quarters of the earth.* (Isa 11:12)

> *Do not be afraid, for I am with you; I will bring your children from the east and* **gather** *you from the west.* (Isa 43:5)

> *"Hear the word of the LORD, O nations; proclaim it in distant coastlands: 'He who scattered Israel will* **gather** *them and will watch over his flock like a shepherd.'"* (Jer 31:10)

> *"This is what the Sovereign LORD says: I will take the Israelites out of the nations where they have gone. I will* **gather** *them from all around and bring them back into their own land."* (Ezek 37:21)

The promise became Israel's prayer:

> *Save us, O LORD our God, and **gather** us from the nations, that we may give thanks to your holy name and glory in your praise.* (Ps 106:47)

The day would come when God would again "gather." The concept of "unity" implicit in the notion of gathering is made explicit by Ezekiel:

> *I will place over them **one** shepherd, my servant David, and he will tend them; he will tend them and be their shepherd. (Ezek 34:23)*

> *I will make them **one** nation in the land, on the mountains of Israel. There will be **one** king over all of them and they will never again be two nations or be divided into two kingdoms.* (Ezek 37:22)

In other words, God's people will again be "one."

Furthermore this "gathering" will embrace not only the people of Israel, but the nations:

> *At that time they will call Jerusalem The Throne of the LORD, and **all nations will gather** in Jerusalem to honor the name of the LORD. No longer will they follow the stubbornness of their evil hearts.* (Jer 3:17)

This promise anticipates the fulfilment of the promise to Abraham that "all nations will be blessed through him" (Gen 18:18). This blessing involves the gathering of people to the throne of the Lord. In this gathering the unity of humanity will be restored, under one King.

The gospel of Jesus Christ announces that the fulfilment of this promise has come. We turn now to explore the relationship between this promised unity and the gospel.

2. Unity and the gospel of Jesus Christ

So far we have seen that unity is God's will for human beings. Human "comm*unity*" has been lost due to sin. This is the story of the human race, as it was the story of Old Testament Israel. However, in faithfulness to his purpose, God promised to "gather" his people, to bring them under one shepherd, to make them again "one."

The gospel of Jesus Christ proclaims that this unity has become a reality, as is the instrument by which God brings this unity into human experience.

The connection between the death of Jesus and the promises of the Old Testament prophets is made unintentionally by the high priest, Caiaphas, when he said to the Sanhedrin "it is better for you that one man die for the people than that the whole nation perish." John comments:

> *He did not say this on his own, but as high priest that year he prophesied that Jesus would die for the Jewish nation, and not only for that nation but also for the scattered children of God, **to bring them together** and make them **one**.* (Jn 11:51-52)

On the night before his death Jesus prayed for this unity (Jn 17:23). The unity Jesus prayed for is the unity the prophets promised, the unity God purposed from creation and the unity that would be brought about by Jesus' death. The gospel, "the word of the cross," is at the same time the word of this unity. How is unity connected to Jesus' death?

The gospel proclaims unity

The gospel proclaims that the unity has been established by the death of Christ. We have now traced the Biblical theme of unity from the beginning of Genesis to this point. The whole Bible leads to the news of the unity that has now been established by an act of God in the death of Jesus Christ.[7]

The New Testament explains that this unity breaks down all of the barriers that have divided the human race: race barriers (Jew and Greek), socio-economic barriers (slave and free), gender barriers (male and female):

> *There is neither Jew nor Greek, slave nor free, male nor female, for you are all* **one** *in Christ Jesus.* (Gal 3:28)

The most significant of these barriers was that between Jew and Gentile. This was deeper than merely ethnic difference. We have seen that God himself put a separation between his people, the Jews (Israel) and other nations. With the overcoming of this division in humanity, a radically new human unity has been made possible. The apostle Paul explains:

> *For he himself is our peace, who has made the two [Jew and Gentile]* **one** *and has destroyed the barrier, the dividing wall of hostility, by abolishing in his flesh the law with its commandments and regulations. His purpose was to create in himself* **one new man** *out of the two, thus making peace, and in this one body to reconcile both of them to God through the cross, by which he put to death their hostility. He came and preached peace to you who were far away [Gentiles] and peace to those who were near [Jews].* **For through him we both have access to the Father by one Spirit.** (Eph 2:14-18)

By the death of Jesus, God has acted to create a new humanity, whose unity is based where human unity began, in coming together before the one God.

The unity that matters is the unity that is the subject of the gospel. We must work out what *that* unity is. How is it expressed? What are its implications? We must take care not to confuse this unity with other kinds of human relationship. Church organisations working well together may have nothing to do with the unity of the gospel. All too often church people can get on very well with one another without ever discovering the unity of which the gospel speaks.

More than this, the gospel not only tells us of the act of God by which he has destroyed the fundamental barriers to human unity. The gospel is also the instrument by which God calls men

---

[7] See J.I. Packer, "The Doctrine and Expression of Christian Unity," *Churchman* 80(1966), reprinted in *Serving the People of God: The Collected Shorter Writings of J.I. Packer* (Carlisle: Paternoster, 1998).[8]

and women, Jews and Gentiles, slaves and freemen into this unity. Unity is therefore not only a subject of which the gospel speaks, but the goal and outcome of gospel proclamation.

The unity the gospel proclaims

The unity the gospel proclaims is not itself visible now—any more than forgiveness or justification is visible now. It is the unity created by Christ's demolition of the dividing wall of hostility between Jew and Gentile—demolished by his death. It is the unity created by the access we all enjoy to the Father, because of Christ's death, by one Spirit. It is, therefore, "the unity of the Spirit" (Eph 4:3).

This unity is classically described in Eph 4:4-6:

> *There is one body and one Spirit—just as you were called to one hope when you were called—one Lord, one faith, one baptism; one God and Father of all, who is over all and through all and in all.* (Eph 4:4-6)

Here is a concise and clear statement of what constitutes the unity proclaimed in the gospel. It is the unity of those who share one Spirit, who have been called to one hope, who have one Lord, who hold one faith, who have a common baptism (in the Spirit, I take it), who belong to one God and Father. This is the unity of which the gospel of Jesus Christ speaks and into which God calls us by the gospel.

The gospel demands unity

Just as the gospel proclaims forgiveness and then demands forgiveness ("forgiving each other, just as in Christ God forgave you" [Eph 4:32]), so the gospel proclaims unity and then demands unity ("Make every effort to keep the unity of the Spirit through the bond of peace" [Eph 4:3]). That is to say, it demands conduct and behaviour consistent with the reality of the unity proclaimed and into which we have been called.

The unity the gospel demands

In the terms of Ephesians 4, the conduct demanded by the unity of the Spirit is this:

> *Be completely humble and gentle; be patient, bearing with one another in love.* (Eph 4:2)

We find an example of believers who were failing to behave like this in Corinth. The believers in that city were not humble and gentle, nor were they patient with one another, nor did they appear to bear with one another in love. Instead they quarrelled over their relationship to different leaders, and other such matters. Paul's appeal to them was:

> *I appeal to you, brothers, in the name of our Lord Jesus Christ, that all of you agree with one another so that there may be no divisions among you and that you may be perfectly **united** in mind and thought.* (1Cor 1:10)

In order to call them back to such unity, Paul explained again the gospel, the "word of the cross"

(1Cor 1:18ff.). Squabbling over leaders is a denial of the gospel, as are so many other divisions between believers.

The gospel divides

It is very interesting to notice how Paul deals with the squabbling in Corinth. We should not be surprised that he reminds them of the gospel which their divisive conduct is denying. However he does so in such a way that shows not only how the gospel unites, but also how the word of the cross divides.

> *For the message of the cross is foolishness to those who are perishing, but to us who are being saved it is the power of God. (1Cor 1:18)*
>
> *Jews demand miraculous signs and Greeks look for wisdom, but we preach Christ crucified: a stumbling block to Jews and foolishness to Gentiles, but to those whom God has called, both Jews and Greeks, Christ the power of God and the wisdom of God. For the foolishness of God is wiser than man's wisdom, and the weakness of God is stronger than man's strength.* (1Cor 1:22-25)

The word of the cross creates a deep division. It is foolishness to those who are perishing, but it is the power of God to those who are being saved.

Therefore wherever the gospel is proclaimed we must expect not only the new unity created by God's Spirit among those whom God calls, but also division between those who believe the gospel and those to whom it is foolishness, many of whom will be the wise of this age (cf. 1Cor 1:20). Even in the Christian congregation, Paul argues, "No doubt there have to be differences[8] among you to show which of you have God's approval" (1Cor 11:19).[9]

The division the gospel creates

Paul's argument in 1Corinthians 1 is instructive at this point. In response to the problem of divisions in the church at Corinth (verses 10-12), he insists on the unity of Christ (verse 13a), and the priority of the gospel of Christ's death (verses 13b-17). This leads to an extended statement about the intentional divisiveness of the word of the cross (verses 18-25).

In this way he highlights the contrast between the way in which the gospel divides and the way in which the Corinthian believers have created divisions. Their divisions arise out of human

---

[8] Greek *haireseis*. "Here it is roughly synonymous with *schismata*, and must mean something similar: divisions, dissensions, factions." G. Fee, *The First Epistle to the Corinthians*, NICNT (Grand Rapids: Eerdmans, 1987), p.538, note 34.

[9] The interpretation of this verse is debated. I agree with Gordon Fee that Paul "probably sees their present divisions as part of the divine 'testing/sifting' process already at work in their midst. Such 'divisions' are not a good thing, but they are an inevitable part of the Eschaton, which has already been set in motion by Christ." Ibid., pp. 538-539. In contrast, for example, Anthony Thiselton argues that "dissensions are unavoidable" is a maxim appealed to, not by Paul, but by the "strong" at Corinth. A. Thiselton, *The First Epistle to the Corinthians: A Commentary on the Greek Text*, NIGTC (Grand Rapids and Carlisle: Eerdmans and Paternoster, 2000), pp. 858-859.

pride, the very thing made impossible by the word of the cross. These were not gospel divisions. They were man made divisions. They were like the divisions that exist among those who are perishing, to whom the word of the cross is weak and foolish.

The division the gospel creates is between those who are called and those who are not (1Cor 1:24), between those who believe the gospel and those who do not.

The gospel that unites and divides

It follows that the unity the gospel creates will be strengthened by clarity about the content of the gospel. Such clarity will also cause division. The right response to such division is humble prayer and careful persuasion. The goal is agreement in the truth. The wrong response is to be less clear and definite about the points of disagreement in order to preserve "unity."

Of course we must be careful not to be "clear and definite" about matters that are not clear and definite in Scripture. However, we must also resist the temptation to be minimalist doctrinally, only being clear and definite about an ever decreasing area in which we can all agree.

Within the New Testament we can observe that almost every document appears to have been written in order to affirm the truth in the context of refuting particular errors. This is required by the uniting/dividing nature of the gospel. This approach of formulating statements of revealed truth that clearly refute particular errors has been followed by subsequent doctrinal statements. The historic creeds, the Reformation formulations such as the Thirty Nine Articles, various evangelical doctrinal statements all reflect the time of their composition, not so much in the truth they affirm as in the particular errors they are at pains to reject.

Those who claim to love the gospel must clearly state its truth in such a way as to unite those who believe it and divide those who do not believe it. The modern phenomenon of formulating statements that can, by virtue of their studied ambiguity, be agreed on by persons who do not agree is a failure to accept the nature of the gospel. The so-called unity that such documents express is an illusion, and gives us no help at all in the important work of addressing our divisions with humble, prayerful persuasion.

3. The evangelical quest for "unity"

The unity which is proclaimed and demanded by the gospel is a key to unravelling at least some of the present evangelical confusion.

There are many recent analyses of "evangelicalism" that are bewildered by the diversity that now calls itself "evangelical." There are various attempts to describe evangelical Christianity by observing the characteristics of those who accept that label. David Bebbington's description is one of the most widely accepted:

"There are four qualities that have been the special marks of Evangelical religion:

conversionism, the belief that lives need to be changed; activism, the expression of the gospel in effort; biblicism, a particular regard for the Bible; and what may be called crucicentrism, a stress on the sacrifice of Christ on the cross. Together they form a quadrilateral of priorities that is the basis of Evangelicalism."[10]

Whatever value there no doubt is in this kind of "objective" description, I would suggest that it is not the *evangelical* understanding of evangelicalism. From the inside an evangelical understands the evangelical "movement" (and I am not sure that is the right word) to be centred on the gospel, the biblical gospel, the only gospel (Gal 1:6-9). It was the gospel that drew people from various backgrounds and traditions and denominations together. I do not dispute the truthfulness of Bebbington's description, as far as it goes. However, an evangelical must insist that the things he mentions are nothing other than the necessary outworking of the gospel of Christ, which *of course* is focused on the cross, and which *of course* we have learnt from the Bible, and which *of course* demands the effort of obedience, and which *of course* calls for and promises changed lives. Evangelical religion is the religion brought into being and shaped by the gospel. It is (as evangelicals have always claimed) authentic, apostolic, New Testament Christianity.

Does this mean that evangelicals agree on everything? No. However what unites evangelicals has always been, and must always be, the gospel. Only the gospel he or she believes gives a person the right to claim to be "evangelical." There is plenty of room for diversity of practice among us in things that we all agree are unimportant. But we must never put the gospel itself, or aspects of the gospel, in that category. That is the danger at the present time.

The history of evangelicalism is not the history of the use of that *word*, but the history of the gospel itself. We recognise a very significant rediscovery of the gospel in the 16th century Reformation. However we do not believe that evangelicalism began there. We thank God for the marvellous and extraordinary impact of the gospel in the 18th century on both sides of the Atlantic. But the gospel preached by Wesley, Whitfield and Edwards had been at work since the day of Pentecost. Wherever that gospel is preached and wherever it is believed, there is evangelicalism. That is the evangelical understanding of evangelicalism.

It is a lamentable but obvious fact of relatively recent history (let us say, the last 50 years or so) that groups and organisations, associations and denominations which came into being under the influence of the gospel, and therefore rightly called themselves "evangelical," have become remarkably diverse, not just in practices that all agree are unimportant, but in theology. Understandings of the gospel have become extraordinarily different among those who still use the label "evangelical."

---

[10] D. Bebbington, *Evangelicalism in Modern Britain: A History from the 1730s to the 1980s* (Grand Rapids: Baker, 1992), pp. 2-3; frequently cited. For example: M. Noll, *American Evangelical Christianity: An Introduction* (Oxford: Blackwell, 2001), p. 13; S.J. Grenz, *Renewing the Center: Evangelical Theology in a Post-Theological Era* (Grand Rapids: Baker, 2000), p. 15.

This diversity is misunderstood if it is seen as variations within one "movement" called "evangelical." We must come to terms with the sorry fact that the diversity is in significant part (at least) the result of persons, organisations and associations moving *away from* the gospel. In reality (despite the retention of the label) there has been movement in various directions away from evangelicalism.

At least that is how I believe it must be seen by gospel people, that is, evangelicals. If this is true, it is a crisis which must be addressed urgently and honestly.

Unity in agreement

David Wells has proposed an hypothesis which may help us to see what has happened.[11] He argues that from the early 1940s through to the 1970s evangelicals (British and American) sought to define themselves *doctrinally*, that is, in terms of *truth*, (in my words) *gospel truth*. This was a period in which a number of very significant personalities had a great impact on evangelicals in both countries: Billy Graham, Carl Henry, John Stott, James Packer. These men were united in their agreement. Although they did not agree on every point of theology, what united them was what they did agree about. And their agreement was substantial. Their influence helped evangelicals to see themselves *confessionally* (to use David Wells' term), to be people united by the one gospel.

It is this understanding of evangelicalism which motivated the drafting of doctrinal statements as the basis for and expression of gospel unity. Such statements attempted to express the truth in a way that united those who believed it, but would be rejected by those who did not believe the same gospel.

The significance of *this* unity is often misconceived by studies of the "evangelical movement." It is treated as a sociological phenomenon. Evangelicals are seen as a group or a "movement" that, like all "movements," had something in common. In this case it was a set of religious beliefs called "the gospel." NO! The unity evangelicals believed they shared was the unity of which the gospel spoke, it was the unity for which Jesus prayed, the unity for which he died. Unity *in* the gospel is the unity *of* the gospel! The unity expressed by shared faith in the one gospel is of an utterly different order from any other kind of unity because it is the unity that the gospel itself creates! It is the unity the gospel is *about*! It is the unity intended by God from the beginning and that will be seen in the end as we gather before his throne.

Unity despite disagreement

Wells suggests that in the late 1970s, as a result of the "success" of the evangelicals, a discernible shift began to take place "from confessional substance to simple organisational fraternity."

---

[11] D. Wells in "On Being Evangelical: Some Theological Differences and Similarities," in M.A. Noll, D.W. Bebbington and G.A. Rawlyk, eds, *Evangelicalism: Comparative Studies of Popular Protestantism in North America, the British Isles, and Beyond, 1700-1990* (New York, Oxford: OUP, 1994), pp. 389-410.

Evangelicals had become an organisation of sorts, a kind of bureaucracy, and to be somewhere within this "righteous empire" was to be evangelical. "Evangelical" had become the name of a "movement."

This is the period in which a very substantial body of Anglican evangelicals in Britain had been rethinking their relationship to the Church of England, and therefore also to non-Anglican evangelicals. The second National Evangelical Anglican Congress (NEAC 2) was held in 1977 in Nottingham. Here the subject of visible church unity was considered, and the view was expressed that significant steps could be taken even if there was a "low degree of doctrinal unity."[12] In a similar, though different, way in the United States the evangelicalism sometimes called "neo" had successfully distanced itself from what was called "fundamentalism," and was engaging with the wider "church" world, from a position of perceived strength. In both cases the doctrinal unity of evangelicals was becoming secondary to other kinds of "unity."

Evangelicals were becoming less conscious of being united by a gospel that distanced them from others. As evangelicals sought to influence the denominations and other organisations in which they found themselves, the importance of theological belief was being displaced by the importance of such things as effective strategy.[13] An institutional mindset was emerging. A concept of unity was emerging that did not depend on doctrinal agreement.

Unity in experience

In the early 1960s another shift was taking place which complicated the picture through the emergence of the charismatic movement. Wells proposes that in this movement theological confession is secondary to what is understood to be the *experience* of the Holy Spirit. This experience unites those of various doctrinal beliefs, whether Catholic or Protestant.

The charismatic movement came to be seen to have "a particular ecumenical significance."[14] Objections to this perception have occasionally been heard. For example:

> "By now it should be generally realized that the major misgivings concerning the charismatic movement in evangelical circles are not phenomenological (i.e. does glossolalia have a place in the church today?) but doctrinal and pastoral. ... Everyone must surely know by now that the charismatic inter-communion services, which are surely the most important feature of this 'ecumenical significance', are only possible because the participants are willing to ignore doctrinal issues and (in the case of Roman Catholics) the laws of their church as well."[15]

---

[12] J. Capon, op. cit., p. 84.
[13] D. Wells, op. cit., p. 391-392.
[14] *The Nottingham Statement: The official statement of the second National Evangelical Anglican Congress held in April 1977* (London: CPAS, 1977), p. 41. Cf. J. Capon, op. cit., pp. 58-64.
[15] Gerald Bray, quoted by J. Capon, op. cit., p. 64.

The contribution of the charismatic movement to a concept of unity that is doctrinally minimalist is difficult to deny.

If Wells is right (and I must say he seems to me to be at least *roughly* right) and if the comments I have made are on the right general track, we have a crisis on our hands. If we have rightly understood the biblical material, we *must* recover a sense of gospel unity *and* gospel division. God is uniting people by the gospel, and dividing people by the gospel. If we are not committed to *that* unity, and, yes, *that* division, we have ceased to be gospel people. We no longer have the right to the name "evangelical" (though that would be the least of our worries!).

II.
Unity: One Church

1. The "ecumenical" dream

As a prisoner for the Lord, then, I urge you to live a life worthy of the calling you have received. Be completely humble and gentle; be patient, bearing with one another in love. Make every effort to keep the unity of the Spirit through the bond of peace. There is one body and one Spirit—just as you were called to one hope when you were called—one Lord, one faith, one baptism; one God and Father of all, who is over all and through all and in all. (Ephesians 4:1-6)

Ecumenical and evangelical "movements" in the 20th century

The ecumenical movement is defined by *The Oxford Dictionary of the Christian Church* as "The movement in the Church towards the recovery of the unity of all believers in Christ, transcending differences of creed, ritual and polity." The modern ecumenical movement is generally understood to owe much to the Evangelical revivals of the 18th and 19th centuries, which so powerfully crossed national and denominational boundaries.

However, through the 20th century the ecumenical movement and evangelicals have taken very different paths. Put simply, but I do not believe unfairly, the focus of the ecumenical movement has been on visible unity of an organisational kind; the focus of the evangelicals has been on the gospel, which both unites and divides.

In time those who call themselves "evangelicals' have become more and more disparate. As we have seen, evangelicalism came to understand itself less "confessionally," because at the level of doctrine there was less agreement. The search was then on (and is still on) for an understanding of evangelicalism, which could embrace a wide spectrum of doctrinal belief, Christian practice and spiritual experience. The evangelical "movement" began to tread the path already traversed by the ecumenical movement, about half a century behind.

In some ways this was a consequence of success. When evangelicalism was small and institutionally weak, it was easy enough for it to be united around shared belief in a common gospel. As more and more people have identified with evangelicalism, and as evangelicalism has in fact come to numerically dominate many of the institutions and to occupy positions of responsibility in them, the uniting power of agreed belief has become difficult. Disagreements are inevitable. We are human. The more of us there are the more disagreements there will be, and as time passes the deeper some of these will become. It is natural then to look for doctrinal agreement in a smaller and smaller area, to become doctrinally minimalist, and to seek substantial unity elsewhere. But where?

Evangelicalism and the doctrine of the church

With the dissipation of evangelicalism there has been a tendency for denominational allegiance to become more important. Logically, if what I have in common with fellow evangelicals becomes less and less, then what I have in common with evangelicals from the same ecclesiastical tradition becomes more and more important. Once I might have thought of myself as an evangelical Christian, identified as such by the gospel I believe, who (by the way) belongs to a church which (as it happens) is linked to the Anglican denomination. But now I am likely to call myself an *Anglican* evangelical, because I share so much more with my fellow Anglican evangelicals than I share with the evangelicals who now seem to have so little in common. Then it is a small step to realise that what we Anglican evangelicals have in common is largely shared by Anglicans who are not evangelicals. I can understand and relate to other Anglicans so much better than I can understand some evangelicals. And so I will think of myself as an evangelical *Anglican* and the lines of relationship that matter most to me have subtly moved from the gospel evangelicals once believed to a particular ecclesiastical tradition, namely in my case Anglicanism.[16]

The time eventually comes when the Anglican evangelicals (who are now evangelical Anglicans!) plan a national conference. They decide to invite a leading Anglican to address them, not on the basis of his evangelical convictions (which he does not have), but on the basis of his office in the denomination. The speaker calls on evangelicals to develop their pitifully weak *ecclesiology*. They admit to their shame that they have not developed an adequate doctrine of the church, and commit themselves to making up for the neglect. That (as I understand it) is what happened at the second and third National Evangelical Anglican Congresses in 1977 (NEAC 2) and 1988 (NEAC 3).[17]

Is anyone then surprised that an ecclesiology begins to emerge which believes in a church united not by creed, but by practice? The official statement of NEAC 2 includes: "The church on earth is

---

[16] This realignment of evangelical self consciousness is, I believe, reflected in the general stance of the collection of essays, *Evangelical Anglicans*, ed. R.T. France and A.E. McGrath (London: SPCK, 1993). Note, in particular, the essay by A. McGrath, "Evangelical Anglicanism: A Contradiction in Terms?" (pp. 10-20), where Evangelicalism and Anglicanism are regarded as "symbiotic, combining to provide an environment in which the inherent dynamism of evangelicalism can be harnessed and more effectively directed through the catholic structures of the Church of England." (pp. 19-20)

[17] At the second National Evangelical Anglican Congress at Nottingham in 1977 the Archbishops of Canterbury and York (Donald Coggin and Stuart Blanch) were invited to speak. At the third such gathering in 1988 at Caister the Archbishop of Canterbury, Robert Runcie, was on the platform. While Archbishops Coggin and Blanch had evangelicalism somewhere in their backgrounds, and might be thought to be 'sympathetic,' this was not the case with Archbishop Runcie. See I. Murray, *Evangelicalism Divided: A Record of Crucial Change in the Years 1950-2000* (Edinburgh: Banner of Truth, 2000), pp. 108-109, 272. In a similar spirit the collection of essays, *Evangelical Anglicans*, concludes with "Evangelicalism: An Outsider's Perspective" by Richard Holloway a leading anglocatholic, and definite non-evangelical.

marked out by Baptism, which is the complete sacramental initiation into Christ and his body.[18] You can now hear some "evangelical Anglicans" referring to the bishop as a symbol of the church's unity! This is a scandal! Ignatius, not Scripture, is shaping our doctrine of the church!

We need to retrace our steps. This is not because the past is always best, and everything was right once. It is because the so-called evangelical movement has lost its way. On the particular question of the doctrine of the church we were deceived if we accepted that evangelicalism lacked an ecclesiology. Perhaps we did not call it an "ecclesiology," and certainly what we had would be judged by many non-evangelicals to be inadequate. I do not doubt that our understanding of the church, like our understanding of anything else, especially something so magnificently wonderful as the church of God, is less than it might be. But did people who believed the biblical gospel fail to believe in the church? Did people who understood the gospel not profoundly understand the church? Just as there is a godly idea of unity and an ungodly one, so there is the church that Jesus Christ is building and there is the church of Babylon. To confuse the two is catastrophic.

What follows is an attempt to explore some aspects of the evangelical doctrine of the church. Then we will explore implications for an evangelical understanding of the denomination.

2. The gospel builds one church

In the region of Caesarea Philippi Jesus conducted a crucial conversation with his disciples concerning his own identity. The details of the conversation are reported by Matthew, Mark and Luke.[19] Matthew provides the fullest record of the words of this conversation.[20] In response to Jesus' question "But what about you? Who do you say I am?", Peter replied "You are the Christ, the Son of the living God" (Matt 16:16). Jesus declared that Peter had come to this knowledge by revelation from "my Father in heaven." In this context he went on to declare "I will build my church" (Matt 16:18).[21] The gates of Hades will not overcome this church.

As reported by Matthew, this conversation has important echoes of the words spoken by God through the prophet Nathan to David in 2Samuel 7.[22] This is the promise on which the messianic expectation of the Old Testament substantially rests. God would raise up a son of David "and I will establish his kingdom" (2Sam 7:12). The text adds: "He is the one *who will build a house for*

---

[18] *The Nottingham Statement*, p. 19. See the documented discussion of the development of a "new" evangelical doctrine of the church in Murray, *Evangelicals Divided*, pp. 99-111

[19] Matt 16:13-20; Mk 8:27-30; Lk 9:18-21.

[20] For a persuasive argument for the historicity of Matthew's additional details see B.F. Meyer, *The Aims of Jesus* (London: SCM, 1979), pp. 184-197.

[21] For our purposes here there is no need to discuss the much debated phrase "on this rock." For a brief survey of views see D.A. Carson, "Matthew," *The Expositor's Bible Commentary*, vol 8 (Grand Rapids: Zondervan, 1984), p.368. In my view, despite the mixture of metaphors involved, "this rock" refers to Jesus himself, who would then be both the builder and the foundation of the church.

[22] On this see B.F. Meyer, *The Aims of Jesus*, pp. 185-197.

my Name, and I will establish the throne of his kingdom forever" (2Sam 7:13). Furthermore "I will be his father, and he shall be my son" (2Sam 7:14).

In the first place this promise points to Solomon. He was the son of David, whose kingdom was established (1Kings 2:46b) and who built the Temple in Jerusalem (1Kings 6). However, Solomon's kingdom did not last, and on the basis of the promise of 2Samuel 7 the prophets spoke of a coming Son of David, who would be God's son and whose kingdom would be forever.[23]

When Peter identified Jesus as the Christ, the Son of God, Jesus announced his task in terms that remind us of the foundational messianic promise "I will build *my church*." He is the son of David who is the Son of God who will build a house for God's name: he will build *his church*.

The church that Jesus is building, therefore, corresponds to the Old Testament temple as type to antitype, shadow to substance, promise to fulfilment. The destruction of Solomon's temple by the Babylonians in 587 BC, and the prophets' promises of a new temple (most strikingly Ezek 40-48, but also many other promises that God will "rebuild"), as well as the rebuilding of the temple and the walls of Jerusalem in the days of Ezra and Nehemiah are in the background of Jesus' promise: "*I will build* my church."

What, then is this "church," and how is the Lord Jesus "building" it?

We notice immediately that the word itself, "church" (Greek *ekklesia*), indicates that what Jesus will "build" is not a material structure such as the Jerusalem temple had been. "Church" (*ekklesia*) means a gathering, an assembly of people. The widespread New Testament use of "building" vocabulary applied to the church is metaphorical.[24]

For example, Paul committed the Ephesian elders "to God and the word of his grace, which is able *to build*" (Acts 20:32).[25] His preaching of the gospel was "building" work (Rom 15:20). The believers in Corinth are "God's building" (1Cor 3:9). Paul described himself as an "expert builder" who in Corinth laid the foundation, namely Jesus Christ. Others were "building" on it. But each had better be careful how he builds. He must measure his building work by the one and only foundation (1Cor 3:10-11). The Corinthians are urged to "seek to abound in the building of the church" (1Cor 14:12). Paul's apostolic authority was given for that task of "building" (2Cor 10:8; 13:10).

The essential background to the metaphor appears to be not simply Jesus' words about building his church, but the widely attested Old Testament promise of a latter day temple. The "building"

---

[23] For example Isa 9:6-7; 11:1-9; Dan 2:44; 7:14. Cf. Ps 2, especially verses 6-9.

[24] Note that the extent of "building" words associated with the church in the New Testament is somewhat obscured in most English translations by two features. Firstly the English often adds the preposition "up" to the verb "build" (with no justification in the Greek which simply has the verb *oikodomeo*). To "build up" in modern English has a misleading psychological/emotional connotation which the simple "to build" lacks. Similarly the verb *oikodomeo* is often translated "edify," which again conveys a subjective sense missing from "build."

[25] NIV has "build *you up*." See previous note.

work is gospel preaching. The "building" itself is the consequence of gospel preaching, namely the church.

In a mixture of metaphors Paul describes the result of the building work:

> *Consequently, you [Gentile believers] are no longer foreigners and aliens, but fellow citizens with the saints [Jewish believers] and members of God's household, built on the foundation of the apostles and prophets [i.e. the foundation laid by the apostles and prophets], with Christ Jesus himself as the chief cornerstone. In him the whole building is joined together and rises to become a holy temple in the Lord. And in him you too are being built together to become a dwelling in which God lives by his Spirit.* (Eph 2:19-22)

Here we have "members of God's household," "the whole building," "a holy temple," "a dwelling." The question remains: What is the reality to which these expressions refer? Where is this household, this building, this temple? What and where is the church that Jesus is building?

The church is the gathering God is gathering to himself

The passage from Ephesians quoted above is set in a context that answers these questions. The various metaphors in Eph 2:19-22 represent the reality that is consequent upon verse 18:

> *For through him [Christ] we both [Gentile and Jew] have access to the Father by one Spirit.* (Eph 2:18)

God's household, this holy temple, consists of Jews and Gentiles because:

> *His purpose was to create in himself one new man out of the two, thus making peace, and in **this one body** to reconcile both of them to God through the cross, by which he put to death their hostility.* (Eph 2:15b-16)

The "building," the "temple," the "household," and many other expressions in the New Testament (including "church") refer to the gathering God is gathering to himself. The Greek word *ekklesia* ("church") translates the Hebrew *kahal*. The Old Testament recalled "the day of the *kahal*," "the day of the assembly," when God brought the people to himself at Mount Sinai (Dt 9:10; 10:4; 18:16 cf. 5:22). We saw earlier how the Old Testament recounts how Israel was eventually "scattered" as a result of their apostasy. The prophets promised that God would one day again "gather." The "church" is the gathering God is now gathering to himself in fulfilment of that promise.

The gospel announces the fulfilment of God's promises, and the "church" is the consequence. It is called in Hebrews 12 "the heavenly Jerusalem," "the city of the living God," "the church of the firstborn, whose names are written in heaven." And it is to this church that the readers of Hebrews 12 are said to "have come." We might therefore regard the word "church" in this sense as itself a metaphor for those who have come into the relationship to God of "sons," those in whom God's Spirit now dwells, those who by that Spirit have the same access to God.

This church is real, and our membership of it is as real as our acceptance by God. However, it is not a physical or visible reality. Like the forgiveness of sins it is known by faith. The historic creeds appear to recognise this:

> "I *believe* in … the holy catholic church; the communion of saints; the forgiveness of sins …" (Apostles' Creed)

> "We believe in the Holy Spirit … We *believe* in one holy catholic and apostolic church." (Nicene Creed)

This church is not to be identified with, and is in no way dependent upon, any institution in this world. Jesus is building this church on the foundation already laid, and "the gates of Hades will not overcome it" (Matt 16:18).

Peter was referring to this church (without using the word "church") when he wrote to "God's elect *scattered* through Pontus, Galatia, Cappadocia, Asia and Bithynia" (1Pet 1:1):

> *As you come to him, the living Stone—rejected by men but chosen by God and precious to him—you also, like living stones, are being built into* **a spiritual house** *to be a holy priesthood, offering spiritual sacrifices acceptable to God through Jesus Christ.* (1Pet 2:4-5)

The scattered believers did not belong to any physical gathering or organisation in this world. Possibly many of them had never met. Nevertheless they belonged together by virtue of having come to Christ, the living capstone. They were being built into the one "spiritual house" (*oikos pneumatikos*).

One of the most remarkable New Testament metaphors for this reality is that of the "body." I do not propose to explore that image in detail now, but to note that when Paul says in Eph 4:4 "There is *one body* …," he must, it seems to me, be referring to this spiritual reality. This is the "body of Christ," which *has been* made holy and clean by Christ's own death "for her" (Eph 5:25-26) and which he will present to himself, holy and blameless (Eph 5:27).

This is "the Holy City, the new Jerusalem" which John saw "coming down out of heaven from God, prepared as a bride beautifully dressed for her husband" (Rev 21:2).

In sum: the church that Jesus is building is a spiritual and eschatological reality, referred to in the New Testament by various expressions. It is the gathering that God is gathering to himself by his Spirit as the gospel is preached.

This church is the end, not a means to an end

Understood this way, it follows that this church is the *end*, the *goal* of God's purposes, not a means to some other end.

Put another way, the church is what *results* from the preaching of the gospel of Jesus Christ in the power of the Spirit, rather than being the *instrument* or *agent* of that preaching (or some other task). The work of the gospel is the building of this church. This church does not therefore have a "mission." The common expression "the mission of the church" needs to be rethought. The church is itself the end product of God's mission. This church is not being built in order to carry our some other task—beyond serving before the throne of God day and night (Rev 7:15).

This church is where the unity of mankind, which was the purpose of the creator from the beginning, is re-established on its proper foundation.

A denomination is not a church

If this is the church of Jesus Christ, it is only confusing for a *denomination* to call itself a "church." Later we will try to explore exactly what a denomination is and what it is for. At this point we should be very clear that words and expressions for "church" in the New Testament are never used for anything remotely like what we call a denomination.

Put simply the Church of England is not a "church," not in any New Testament sense of that word and not in any theologically significant sense of the word. The same, of course, must be said of the Baptist, Presbyterian, Lutheran and Roman Catholic "churches."

It is important to see that this is more than a semantic debate. After all, words develop various meanings over time, and any English dictionary will tell you that one of the meanings of the word "church" is an organisation like the Church of England. The point I am making, however, is that *that* meaning of "church" is not found in the Bible, and it is a completely non-theological usage. That is to say, the entity we call the Church of England is, as such, of no theological significance at all. We must not attribute to the denomination (as such) any of the significance the New Testament gives to the church.

The church that Jesus Christ is building is a different kind of thing altogether from a denomination. However, it is not "a different kind of thing altogether" from something else. The something else is what we must now see.

3. The church is "seen" in the gathering of believers

When the gospel comes to a locality, by an evangelist, or by a believer who moves there, as it is heard, through personal testimony or gospel preaching, one, two or more may be converted as God calls them to himself in repentance and they put their faith in the Lord Jesus Christ. As they come to God through Christ, they are being built into his church. And, at the same time, since they are in the same locality they are drawn into fellowship with one another by God's Holy Spirit who indwells them.

When these members of God's household, who now share the one Holy Spirit, who are now sons of the one Father, come together into one another's company, to meet with each other, to meet together with their Lord, to continue to be built into the church that Jesus is building as they speak the word of Christ to one another, *there* you get a glimpse of the church that Jesus is building. There that church can be "seen."[26]

It is not the church because it is 11 am on Sunday morning, and the notice board outside announces that "church" is on at that time! The gathering of believers is the church because it is the gathering of those *in that place* whom God has gathered (and is gathering) to himself.

The local gathering is therefore called "the church of God as it is in Corinth" (1Cor 1:2), "the church at Antioch" (Acts 13:2), and so on. Those who mistreat members of the church in Corinth "despise the church of God" (1Cor 11:22). The significance of the local gathering lies in the spiritual reality of which it is an expression in time and space. The Ephesian elders, as they cared for the church in their city, were shepherds of "the church of God which he bought with his own blood" (Acts 20:28).

P.T. Forsyth captured this point like this:

> "It is not strictly correct to speak of the Corinthian Church, but of the Church of Corinth, as it comes to the surface there. And the Church in a private house was as much the Church as the whole Christian community of Corinth."[27]

The most common use of the word "church" in the New Testament is in reference to local gatherings of believers. In this sense, of course, there are many "churches." There are many places where God has gathered people to himself. However, when these local gatherings are referred to collectively, they are not "the church," but, for example, "the church*es* of God" (1Cor 11:16). The word "church" in the singular applies either to the one church, the spiritual house, which is not seen, or a local gathering in a particular place. The common modern expression "the New Testament *church*" or "the early *church*," where the singular "church" is used collectively for the church*es* of the period has no parallel in any New Testament writer. The small number of apparent exceptions to this are, on closer examination, not exceptions at all.[28]

---

[26] Cf. D.B. Knox, "Denomination and Society," in B.G. Webb, ed., *Explorations 3* (Homebush West: Lancer, 1988), pp. 97-98.

[27] P.T. Forsyth, *The Church and the Sacraments* (London, 1947 ed.), cited in J.I. Packer, "The Doctrine and Expression of Christian Unity," *Churchman* 80(1966), reprinted in *Serving the People of God: The Collected Shorter Writings of J.I. Packer* (Carlisle: Paternoster, 1998), p. 37.

[28] See D.W.B. Robinson, "Church," in *The Illustrated Bible Dictionary*, Part 1 (Leicester: IVP, 1980), pp. 283-286. The few apparent exceptions to this rule, according to Robinson, are all references to the Jerusalem church "throughout the first generation it was 'the church' *par excellence*" (so Acts 9:31; 18:22; 1Cor 15:9; Gal 1:13; Phil 3:6). See how Paul impressed this perspective on his churches in Rom 15:27.
On Acts 9:31, notice that this verse concludes the section that began "On that day a great persecution broke out against *the church at Jerusalem*, and all except the apostles were scattered throughout Judea and Samaria" (Acts 8:1). The "church" that by 9:31 was said to enjoy peace, was the Jerusalem church which was now scattered. It was this church that Saul (Paul) "began to destroy" (Acts 8:3). It is consistent, therefore, with the record of Acts to relate Paul's own references to his persecution of "the church" or "the church of God" to the Jerusalem church.

The "visible" and the "invisible" church

The two senses in which I am suggesting the New Testament speaks of the "church" seem very close to the Reformers' distinction between the "visible" and the "invisible" church.

As J.I. Packer has pointed out it is important to understand that the Reformers did not think that they were talking about two churches when they distinguished between the visible and the invisible church: the "real" church which is invisible, and the "visible" church which is not really the church at all. Rather "visible" and "invisible" referred to two aspects of the one church: "that which it wears to the eyes of men, who see only the appearance, and that which it has to the eye of God, who looks on the heart and knows things as they are, and whose estimate of spiritual realities, unlike ours, is unerring."[29]

However, what I am suggesting here is an understanding that goes further than the Reformers in the emphasis that the "visible" church is the actual gathering of believers in a particular place.

It is not surprising that those who hold that the stuff of ecclesiology is order, polity, liturgy, canon law, synods and the like, see evangelicals as holding to an under-developed doctrine of the church. However, the opposite is true. To shift the focus of ecclesiology from the spiritual reality and its local expression in the congregation is to shift attention from the church of God to something quite different.

When is a church a church?

When, then, is a church a church? The classic "marks" of the church are an attempt to answer that question. I think that the expression of Article 19 of the Thirty Nine Articles is difficult to improve on:

> "The visible Church of Christ is a congregation of faithful men, in which the pure Word of God is preached, and the Sacraments be duly ministered according to Christ's ordinance in all those things that of necessity are requisite to the same."

A gathering of people of true faith in God is a church. Such a gathering will of necessity have the word of God spoken and will act in accordance to Christ's commands.

The point is that the church is complete wherever two or three have been gathered by God to himself by his word. The trappings that we have added, and now associate with "church" do not add *anything* essential (or even important) to the reality of church. We must stop thinking that the home Bible study group is *less church* than the gathering at 11 am on Sunday. The home Bible Study group, or any other gathering of believers in the name of Christ lacks *nothing of any consequence* as the church of God.

---

[29] J.I. Packer, *op. cit.*, p. 38.

Of course, conversely, a gathering of unbelievers, who have *not* been gathered by God to himself, who are not sons of God, and where the word of God is not heard is not a church no matter how many ecclesiological credentials of "apostolic succession," liturgical magnificence, irreproachable order, and impeccable denominational credentials are claimed. Nothing of the New Testament doctrine of the church applies to such a gathering. It is of no more consequence than a golf club. Indeed it is of markedly less significance, due to its blatant hypocrisy!

What I am presenting is often disparagingly called "congregationalism." How amazing (and inconsistent with Article 19!) that "congregational" has become a negative term! There is no shame in recognising the glory of the gathering that God gathers in each place. The shame is to seek that glory in the institutions of man, where it is not to be found.

What, then, is the "Church of England"?

This does lead us to the question to which we must shortly return: What is the "Church of England"? Theoretically it is an association, a linking, of *some* of the *churches* in England. That is all. The *association* is not the church. You do not see the church that Jesus is building when you see the Church of England. The churches that are associated with each other in this way are not more authentically churches, nor better churches, than those which are not so associated. Nor, may I say, are they worse.

In practice, of course, the Church of England is an association of groups, only some of which are actually churches on the New Testament (or even the Thirty Nine Articles) definition. There are some gatherings which call themselves "churches," where the pure word of God is not heard, and true faith in God is therefore non-existent. These are not really "churches" at all. Part of our dilemma is finding ourselves in an association which some may say has become dominated by such groups. However, once we have seen that the association is not "the church," it is reasonable to ask whether the admittedly regrettable disparity in the "mixed" denominations is as big a problem as some have supposed. That is a question to which we will return.

4. The unity of *this* church is to be "kept"

The point to which this study has been leading is that the church which Jesus is building is the place where the unity which the gospel proclaims is established and it is the place where the unity the gospel demands is to be expressed. In other words, the point at which the idea of Christian unity is usually applied (between denominations, or within denominations) is not nearly as important as applying this reality where it belongs, namely to the church that Jesus is building.

Let us note carefully, in the first place, that the unity of *this* church is not under threat.

The unity in not under threat

In a question time recently after a public lecture, someone asked what I thought about the future of the church. I hesitated, wondering what useful thing could be said in reply to such a broad question. I found myself thinking that I had no idea. The statistics are far from encouraging. The media is against us. The culture is against us. Multiculturalism and tolerance have effectively relativised the claims of the gospel. There is far more community interest in Islam than in Christ.

See how easily our minds lose sight of reality! The true answer to the questioner is that the church that Jesus Christ is building is not under threat. The gates of hell will not prevail against it! Its security has been won by the victory of Christ on the cross over the principalities and powers in the heavenly places.

And likewise the *unity* of this church is not under threat. "You *are* all one in Christ Jesus" (Gal 3:28b). The prayer of Jesus in John 17 has been answered, and is being answered "as you come to him" and are being built as living stones into one spiritual house (1Pet 2:4-5). The dividing walls of hostility have been abolished (Eph 2:14-15).

Do you think that the unity of the church that Jesus is building is threatened by actions or events that might cause havoc in the Church of England? Whether or not causing havoc in the Church of England is a good thing is another question. And it will depend. But it is important for us to know and believe that havoc in the Church or England is not the same thing as threatening the unity of the church. Divisions in the Church of England are no danger to the unity of the church simply because the Church of England is not the church.

To the north of my home in Sydney, just beyond the Anglican diocesan boundary, a young Anglican clergyman from the diocese of Sydney recently planted a church in an area where there is a need for many churches. A number of Sydney parishes supported the project. The hierarchy of the neighbouring diocese was furious, as were most of the Anglican clergy in the area. Why? When it all boiled down, at the heart of the outrage was the fact that an ordained Anglican minister was conducting a ministry in the territory of an Anglican bishop without that bishop's permission and oversight. It was an assault on the unity of the church, you see.

It was no such thing. There was a denominational demarcation dispute. Some Anglicans deeply resented what was done. Some were angry. But there was no threat to the church that Jesus is building. Indeed, in my opinion, the action was a proper and thoroughly appropriate outworking of the unity of Christ's church. It was an action that built the church. We must not confuse peace in the denomination with the unity of the church.

Allowing lay people to administer the Lord's Supper in Anglican churches will, we are told, divide the church. Evangelicals will be marginalised and no longer be listened to. To do something like that would just demonstrate how little evangelicals care about the unity of the church.

That, again, is confused thinking. People being upset, even angry about an action, a proposal, a policy, or a statement is not a threat to the church of Jesus Christ and its unity. After all, has not history shown that the preaching of the gospel itself is likely to encounter such reactions within the denominations? Actions that express gospel truth are sure to meet similar responses because they are (rightly!) perceived to threaten cherished, but false beliefs. It is worth asking: what is it that people believe about the church when they are angered by a church being planted without a bishop's oversight? What beliefs about Christian ministry and the sacraments cause people to oppose lay persons being allowed to lead the prayers at the Lord's Supper?

One difficulty arising from such confused thinking is that denominations have often sought to maintain their unity through enforcing uniformity of practice. The Act of Uniformity of 1662 is a notorious example. This was no way to protect the unity of the church! By this measure large numbers of faithful ministers of the gospel were forced out of the Church of England.[30]

What, then, is the unity of the church? It is this:

> *There is one body and one Spirit—just as you were called to one hope when you were called—one Lord, one faith, one baptism; one God and Father of all, who is over all and through all and in all.* (Eph 4:4-6)

Consider the unity of the church displayed in these words.

"One body." This one body is the church: the one gathering of Jew and Gentile, slave and free, male and female, called by God into his presence by the gospel. The fatal mistake is to think that the one body is some world wide, or even national organisation. There was no such organisation when Paul wrote these words, neither was there any move or reason to establish one. The organisational links that have developed over the centuries must not in any way be confused with this one body. "It is the heavenly gathering, assembled around Christ, in which believers now participate."[31]

When a policy or proposal is criticised as "divisive," it is important to remember the unthreatened unity of the one body.

"One Spirit." On the one hand, we all have access to the Father by one Spirit (Eph 2:18). On the other hand, it is the one Spirit, or breath,[32] indwelling the members that animates the one body. The one body consists of those in whom the one Spirit dwells.

What the one Spirit has united is secure.

"Just as also you were called to one hope when you were called." Paul earlier prayed that "the eyes of your heart may be enlightened in order that you may know the hope to which he has called you, the riches of his glorious inheritance in the saints" (Eph 1:18). The point now, however, is that there is one body because there is one Spirit, and just as there is one Spirit there is one call, one gospel and one gospel hope.

---

[30] For some perceptive insights into this incfident see J.I. Packer, *A Quest for Godliness: The Puritan Vision of the Christian Life* (Wheaton: Crossway Books, 1990), pp. 119-122.
[31] P.T. O'Brien, *The Letter to the Ephesians*, The Pillar New Testament Commentary (Leicester: Apollos, 1999), p.281.
[32] Both the Greek *pneuma* and the Hebrew *ruach* mean both "spirit" and "breath."

"One Lord." That is, the Lord Jesus Christ. The church's unity is as certain as the uniqueness of her one Lord.

"One faith." In this one body there is only one object of faith, and only one proper content of faith. Beware those who glory in theological diversity. There is "one faith." Not one for Jews and one for Gentiles. How much less one for Anglicans and one for free-churches, or one for one party of Anglicans and one for another party. In the one body there is one faith.

"One baptism." Paul was clearly not thinking of our distinction between water and Spirit baptism. Nor is it conceivable that he identified those two things as one and the same. It seems to me certain that he means the baptism in the one Spirit by which all believers, Jews and Greeks, slave and free, were incorporated into one body (cf. 1Cor 12:13).

Finally: "One God and Father of all, who is over all and through all and in all."

This is the unity of the church of God.

The unity is under threat

Only when we see and believe in the unity that is not under threat can we understand properly the fact that the unity is under threat.

This very passage in Ephesians 4 is preceded by the call to "Make every effort [there is a sense of urgency and energy in this word[33]] to *keep* the unity of the Spirit through the bond of peace" (Eph 4:3).

Likewise Paul was dismayed at the news that there were divisions among the believers in Corinth:

> *I appeal to you, brothers, in the name of our Lord Jesus Christ, that all of you agree with one another so that there may be no divisions[34] among you and that you may be perfectly united in mind and thought.* (1Cor 1:10)

And in a kind of mirror image of Ephesians 4 he asks:
> *Is Christ divided[35]? Was Paul crucified for you? Were you baptized into the name of Paul?* (1Cor 1:13)

To the Romans Paul wrote:
> *I urge you, brothers, to watch out for those who cause divisions[36] and put obstacles in your way that are contrary to the teaching you have learned. Keep away from them.* (Rom 16:17)

Where, and in what ways is the unity of the church, which is not under threat, under threat?

---

[33] Greek *spoudazo*.
[34] Greek *schismata*.
[35] Greek *merizomai*.
[36] Greek *dichostasiai*.

This paradox reflects the two aspects of the church we have already noted. The spiritual and eschatological reality itself is secure. However where this reality comes to expression in a particular locality in this world the potential for division is present.

This brings us to the important observation that the divisions that are of concern in the New Testament are located in the local congregation of believers. Likewise the conduct required of believers, in the light of the unity of the church, has to do with behaviour between members of the local congregation. Is it not an interesting fact that the concern about divisions that we find in the New Testament is *all* focused on divisions within the congregation, *not* divisions between congregations?

The behaviour that will "keep" the unity of the Spirit according to Ephesians 4 is the conduct between believers who meet with one another: it is humility towards one another, gentleness in dealing with one another, patience in response to one another, bearing with one another in love (Eph 4:2). Those who cause divisions according to Rom 16 are those whose smooth talk and flattery deceive the minds of naïve people with teaching "contrary to the teaching you have learned" (Rom 16:17-18).

Right thinking about unity is closely related to right thinking about church. The unity that matters is the unity of the church that Jesus is building. The threat to that unity is the possibility of a congregation failing to live and behave in ways that are worthy of the unity that gospel has brought about. Paul's call to unity is introduced by these words:

As a prisoner for the Lord, then, I urge you to live a life worthy of the calling you have received. (Eph 4:1)

"Keep" the unity

The exhortation of Ephesians 4:3 is to "keep" / "maintain" the unity of the Spirit. This unity is "kept" / "maintained" by the way in which believers behave towards each other in the congregation, and the rejection of false teaching in the congregation.

If we are serious about the unity that matters, our focus will be on the health of the local congregation, the church as it is in each place. That is where the unity of the Spirit is displayed, and that is where it is to be "kept."

The "ecumenical movement" was a wrong path from the beginning. The unity that matters is secure: the Lord Jesus Christ is building one church, the reality of which is manifested wherever people are gathered by the gospel. To confuse this unity with the harmony of a human organisation, such as a denomination, is positively Babylonian! Beware of Babylonian church unity. It must not be a guide to our conduct.

With such an understanding of church and unity, is there any significant place for the denomination? To this question we now turn.

III.
Unity and Denominations

1. What is a denomination?

> *Whatever happens, conduct yourselves in a manner worthy of the gospel of Christ. Then, whether I come and see you or only hear about you in my absence, I will know that you stand firm in one spirit, contending as one man [soul] for the faith of the gospel without being frightened in any way by those who oppose you. This is a sign to them that they will be destroyed, but that you will be saved—and that by God. For it has been granted to you on behalf of Christ not only to believe on him, but also to suffer for him, since you are going through the same struggle you saw I had, and now hear that I still have.* (Philippians 1:27-30)

It is immensely reassuring (and more than a little sobering) to hear the apostle speak of "struggle," "suffering," "opposition," "contending" and even "being frightened" in the same breath as "unity" ("one spirit," "one soul"). The unity of which he speaks he expects to be strongly opposed and is worked out only with difficulty. The unity for which Paul contended was opposed, not by out and out pagans, but by what we might call the religious establishment (Judaism) or people who claimed to belong to Christ, yet did not want unity on the basis of the gospel alone.

This, I believe, sets an appropriate tone for our exploration of our third topic: Unity and denominations.

A definition

What is a denomination?

It is commonly suggested that the denomination is a modern phenomenon. Similarly we often hear reference to the period of the "undivided church." Such a reading of history (may I suggest) is superficial.

While the term "denomination" is relatively modern, and the denominations have developed in particular ways in modern times, I want to suggest that *what a denomination fundamentally is* has existed since New Testament times, and has only ceased to exist in times and places where persecution or coercion of some kind has been used as an instrument to prevent it. Denominations are, I am suggesting, an inevitable consequence of the progress of the gospel, and not, in themselves, a cause for concern. On the contrary, evangelicals should welcome and defend the phenomenon of denominations, but also be much clearer than we often are about what a denomination is and what it isn't. I confess to being not only a congregationalist, but also a denominationalist. But since these are usually regarded as mutually exclusive, I have some explaining to do!

Here is a working definition: *A denomination is an **association** of **some churches** which does not include **all churches**.*

The features of a denomination I am including in this definition are:

(a)   It is an *association* of churches, but it is not a church.

(b)   It is an association of *churches*, as distinct from an association of individual Christians.

(c)   It is an association which, in principle, does not include, and does not need to include, all churches.

Put as simply as that, three obvious questions are raised:

(1)   Why would such an association come into existence?

(2)   What kind or kinds of "association" are meant?

(3)   What good purposes could such an association have?

These questions are not answered in the definition offered because a great variety of answers are possible. There are many good and proper reasons for such an association to exist, none of which is essential to the definition. The association may take various forms and achieve a number of good purposes, but no particular denomination needs to attempt them all.

I am not interested here in tracing the use of the *term* "denomination,"[37] which in roughly the sense employed here was popularised in the 18th century by leaders of the Evangelical Revival and the Great Awakening.[38] Suffice to say that in that context (as here) the concept was humble. It implied only that the group referred to shared the "name" given to the association on view. Denominationalism, in this sense, is a deliberate rejection of sectarianism, the view that a particular group is the only legitimate expression of the church.

Denominationalism as a *concept* (as distinct from the terminology) is often traced back to the 17th, or even 16th centuries.[39] However, I suggest that we ought to see that it has been there from the beginning.

"Denominations" in the New Testament?

Within the New Testament we see certain churches sharing an association which did not include all churches. The most obvious example, from the evidence we have, is the so-called Pauline

---

[37] "Denomination," from the verb "denominate," originally meant "the action of giving a name to." It came to refer to a collection of individuals classed under the same name. The first use of the term in this sense recorded by *The Oxford English Dictionary* was in 1716.

[38] See W.S. Hudson, "Denominationalism," *The Encyclopedia of Religion*, ed. M. Eliade, vol 4 (New York & London: Macmillan and Collier Macmillan, 1987), p. 293. Also S.J. Grenz, *Renewing the Center: Evangelical Theology in a Post-Theological Era* (Grand Rapids: Baker, 2000), p. 296.

[39] Cf. Hudson, *op. cit.*, p. 293.

churches. These churches had in common their personal link with the founding apostle and evangelist, Paul. Paul's letters and their circulation, his visits and those of his associates, the famous "collection" are all expressions of this association. We note that there was no *organisational link* between these churches. Some were more closely associated than others simply because of their location (Col 4:15-16; 1Thess 4:10). Paul's authority with respect to these churches was real, but not institutionalised (cf. 2Cor 10:8; 13:10), and was exercised by persuasion and exhortation.[40]

There is, of course, nothing inherently wrong with the association of churches who shared this relationship with Paul. Neither is there any basic reason that other churches should or should not be drawn into that association. It does seem that churches like Laodicea and Colossae which were not established by Paul himself, but by those who had themselves been brought the gospel by Paul, were drawn into the association.[41] There is certainly something to be said about the *attitude* of those who belong to the association towards those who do not. The collection for the saints in Jerusalem (emphatically *not* one of the Pauline churches) was an important expression of that.

The potential for disagreements to arise between churches associated on one basis and others associated on another basis is as real as the potential for disagreements within a congregation or between churches that share some association. It is reasonable to suppose (indeed it is difficult to imagine otherwise) that there were churches who did not see eye to eye with the Pauline churches on some matters, indeed some matters of fundamental importance.

Therefore in principle the essential elements of modern denominationalism appear to be recognisable within the New Testament. This is not to suggest that the mere existence of these things in New Testament times justifies or requires their existence today. It does, however, alert us to the fact that our responses to denominationalism may find more direct guidance from the New Testament than we might otherwise have expected.

Denominations in history

History has produced an enormous variety and complexity of associations between churches. Some of these associations have become expressed in complex organisational structures with their own long histories. Various understandings of the significance of these structures have emerged.

Over time the organisational structures have taken on a life of their own. "Anglicanism," for example, has become something valued in its own right. For a wide variety of historical reasons the churches (congregations) associated by the structures have become increasingly diverse in

---

[40] See L.L. Belleville, "Authority, 1. Of Paul," in *Dictionary of Paul and his Letters*, ed. G.F. Hawthorne and R.P. Martin (Leicester and Downers Grove: IVP, 1993), pp. 55-57.
[41] Ibid., p. 57.

faith and practice. Certainly the older denominational structures now include many groups of people where the word of God is never heard, and there is no reason to believe that those who gather have been born again. They are no longer churches of God. Further, the organisational structure as a whole can fall into the hands of people who do not believe the gospel.

The evangelical denominational dilemma

This constitutes the dilemma facing evangelicals in the historic denominations today. There are at least three approaches to the situation:

- There are those who take the view that evangelicals cannot remain in an organisational structure that has utterly lost the gospel, or promotes a false gospel.
- There are those who want to stay in the structure in order to change it back to what it was "originally" meant to be ("reform" is our word!).
- There are those who take the view that the organisation was set up by gospel churches for gospel churches, and there is no way *we* are going to leave.

And there are other views.[42]

I want to address that dilemma in the following way.

First let us reflect on the value and importance of denominationalism. Denominationalism rejects, on the one hand, the desire for one pure association of true churches, and on the other hand congregational independence. I want to argue that denominations can be an expression of the unity of the Spirit.

Then I would like to reflect on some of the difficulties denominations can, and apparently inevitably do cause. These arise from misunderstandings of the nature of a denomination and inappropriate policies and actions by the denominations. I want to consider how a denomination can oppose the unity of the Spirit.

Thirdly I would like to draw some simple implications for evangelicals and evangelical churches and our life with respect to our denominations.

2. A denomination can express the unity of the Spirit

Previously I argued for a congregational understanding of the church (which is a tautology!). By his Spirit through the gospel the Lord is building his church: calling people to himself. In this world the effect of this work is seen as the Lord calls people to himself in various localities. Those drawn by God to himself are drawn by his Spirit to each other. I have argued that the word "church," and the glorious significance of the church of God according to the New

---

[42] For an important analysis of the history of denominationalism and the present crisis, with a particular eye on the Church of England, see D. Holloway, *Church and State in the New Millennium: Issues of Belief and Morality for the 21st Century* (London: Harper Collins, 2000), pp. 221-227.

Testament including the unity of the Spirit, applies to this reality, both in its spiritual, or heavenly, aspect *and* its earthly physical expression, the local gathering of believers.

However, this does *not* imply that in this world congregations should regard themselves as "independent" in the sense of not having relationships with other congregations. Independence, in this sense, is a non-Christian concept. The church of God in Corinth shared the experience of being sanctified in Christ Jesus, of being called, of being holy "with *all* who call on the name of our Lord Jesus Christ in *every* place—their Lord and ours" (see 1Cor 1:2). "The same Spirit which draws us into each other's company to share Christ together will also give us a spirit of love and unity with other congregations as we come to know of their existence."[43]

Fellowship between congregations

The question is, how should the unity we share with believers other than those with whom we meet be expressed? Because of limitations of time and space it is impractical to *meet* with those believers (at least not all of them!). Yet they too are members of the one church that Jesus is building. What expression should be given to that reality?

The answer will vary according to circumstances. There may be opportunities to communicate, to co-operate, to help, to be helped. Physical limitations mean in these ways, too, it will not be possible to relate to *all* other believers. However we will want to express our love and unity with others to the extent that it is feasible.

Such opportunities are likely to especially arise between churches that share common characteristics or common experiences. A special relationship with Paul provided such opportunities in New Testament times. A shared history and way of doing things may provide such opportunities today. However it is highly unlikely that there will be significant opportunities for all believers all over the world to express their fellowship in any meaningful way, simply because of the limitations of the physical world.

The denomination (an association between churches) arises out of the Spirit of fellowship between believers beyond their own congregation, and its purpose is to express and facilitate the fellowship of the Spirit beyond the local congregation.[44]

If a congregation or house church asserts its independence, in the sense that it has no desire to relate to other believers or churches, there is a defective understanding of the church that Jesus is building, and an inadequate experience of "the fellowship of the Holy Spirit" (2Cor 13:14). Such a group tends to become a "club" rather than the church of Christ. A club is a group that exists to satisfy the felt needs of its members rather than being the gathering that God is gathering to himself.[45]

---

[43] D.B. Knox, "Denomination and Society," in B.G. Webb, ed., *Explorations 3* (Homebush West: Lancer, 1988), p. 100.
[44] Ibid., p. 101.
[45] Cf. Ibid.

In the early days of the gospel, this wider fellowship was expressed in relatively unstructured ways, some of which we have noted.

In time structures were developed to advance the fellowship between churches. The first such formal structure of which we know was a meeting between senior church members to resolve a problem that was affecting the life of the churches (Acts 15). While the history books call this "The Council of Jerusalem," that is to project back onto it an official and formal status that developed only later. It was an expression of Christian fellowship between the churches appropriate to the particular need that had arisen.

Structures developed in complexity over the centuries. A permanent central bureaucracy developed. The structures did not necessarily arise or develop in ways consistent with the fellowship of the Spirit. These structures therefore often became problematic, for the purpose of the association must always be remembered: to express and deepen fellowship between churches.

We will return to those problems shortly. First we need to take note of some specific advantages in the denominational way of associating.

Freedom of conscience

One of the features of what we are calling a denomination is that it does not embrace all churches. Discussions of denominations use the expression "parallel denominations" to indicate the existence in one place of several churches each belonging to a different association of churches.

I am suggesting that there have always been (in principle at least) "parallel denominations." The reasons for more than one association of churches, even in one geographical area may be various, but one of them is the inevitable development of conscientious disagreements between believers.

Because we recognise the imperfection of our knowledge and wisdom we do not anticipate complete agreement on all things between all believers in this world. Parallel denominations provide for liberty of conscience. The alternative to parallel denominations is one denomination which could only be maintained by persecution. This was attempted by the medieval Roman Church, and in England by the Church of England with the 1662 Act of Uniformity.

To allow freedom of conscience on certain matters requires parallel associations. These are not necessarily the most important matters, but they are the matters in which disagreement makes practical co-operation of some kind unworkable.

The Church of England, like the Anglican Church of Australia, has not yet resolved the question whether one denomination can cope with opposite views of the ordination of women. This is not because this is the most serious theological issue within the life of the Church of England. It is clear that the Church of England can cope more easily with an enormous range of mutually exclusive views on the atonement and the resurrection than opposite views on the ordination of women.

This is because of the nature of the association that the Church of England happens to be. It involves recognising and accepting ministers. For the first time ministers are being recognised by some in the association whose ministry cannot *in principle* be accepted in conscience by others. If the denomination cannot come to genuine agreement on this matter there are only two ways forward: coercion or the creation of two or more associations either separately or within the broader association. History suggests we will go for coercion! There are clear indications that there are those who are already pressing for this solution. A proper understanding of denomination would be more willing to develop parallel associations within the broader association called the Church of England.

One of the chief benefits of denominationalism (the freedom of conscience it allows) is lost when the denomination resorts to coercion of consciences. The unity of the Spirit cannot be coerced against conscience.

Cooperation

Another obvious benefit of churches associating with one another in denominations is the potential for cooperation in projects that require more resources than those at the disposal of most local congregations.

Examples could include the recruiting and training of ministers, the support of gospel work in difficult areas, the sending and support of overseas missionaries, the publication of literature for use by the churches, the scholarly investigation of issues facing the churches, the provision of joint ownership of property, the provision of retirement support for ministers—and so on.

In principle these different tasks could be explored through different associations. Most of them could be accomplished through the cooperative action of individual Christians, rather than an association of churches. Indeed the support of overseas missions has historically worked well through voluntary societies of Christian people separate from denominational structures. In principle such voluntary societies are very like denominations. They arise out of the fellowship of the Spirit, the unity of the Spirit, beyond the local congregation. Such societies may provide links of fellowship between churches. Then, in principle, they are denominations.

In theory there could be any number of such associations, on different bases for different purposes—and of course there are many in fact. If this is accepted, then we do not only have *parallel* denominations, but *overlapping* denominations. There are the churches which are associated through their support of a particular "interdenominational" missionary agency. This is a denomination across the denominations! In principle such associations are to be welcomed and encouraged so long as they encourage the fellowship and unity of the Spirit.

However a denomination does not always work as it should.

3. A denomination can oppose the unity of the Spirit

A denomination is not a church, and it is dangerous to treat it as though it is. Then the denomination inevitably becomes opposed to the unity of the Spirit, for it confuses its own structures with the unity of God's church.

A church, that is a congregation, is ruled over by God's Spirit through his Word. A denomination, because it rarely (if ever) meets for this purpose, is not under the influence of God's Spirit in the same way as a church is (or should be). It is particularly easy, therefore, for a denomination to lose sight of its proper spiritual role.

Once a denomination has developed institutional structures that people come to think are "the church," the trouble has begun. Instead of being an expression of the unity of the Spirit, an outworking of the fellowship of those who in different places call on the name of our Lord Jesus Christ, the denomination can then impede the fellowship of the Holy Spirit. Indeed history suggests that over time this temptation is close to irresistible.

There is a solemn responsibility on those who belong to such an association to ensure that the association works for good, but is not allowed to quench the Spirit. The denomination is a voluntary association, no matter what power its organisation may have acquired over the years and centuries. The denomination must be understood to be subordinate to the churches belonging to it, not the other way round. And where it has become the other way round, it must be turned back again! Those who voluntarily choose to belong to (or remain in) the association thereby have the responsibility to promote the good the association can achieve, but fight the harm it can do.

Let us consider the potential for the denomination to oppose the unity of the Spirit under three headings: Denominational centralism, Denominational loyalty, and Denominational distinctiveness.

Denominational centralism

If our understanding is approximately correct, the spiritual justification for the denomination is the unity that exists between believers beyond the local congregation. The congregation remains the primary expression of the unity of the Spirit. The relationships created by Christ's demolition of the barriers are most fully manifested in this world in the congregation. That is where we should especially see humility, gentleness, patience and love (Eph 4:2).

The first temptation for the denomination (and I would suggest the first thing that happens once the purpose of the denomination is forgotten) is that the association's central organisation becomes more important than the churches it exists to serve. The denomination becomes a franchise operation, where the local outlets have permission to market the brand-name.

With centralism comes control and interference. Whereas in spiritual reality the local gathering of believers is assembled by Christ, ruled by his Spirit through his Word as the members serve one another, the denomination is tempted to rule the congregation from a distance, and according to its own interests. The greater the control exercised by the central body, the more passive the members of the local congregations become, until they abandon their responsibilities for the church's life, and do not care about faithfulness to Christ and to one another.

I believe that it is urgent and necessary and a grave duty to see that the control of the denomination over the life and ministry of the local congregation must be broken. In the case of a denomination where the values and goals of the association as a whole (and centrally) have lost touch with the biblical gospel, this is absolutely imperative and pressing. Otherwise very soon there will be no place for evangelical ministry in that denomination. The signs are already there for all to see. If we are prepared to accept that outcome we should leave the denomination now. If not, we must act now.

What would it mean to break the control of the denomination over the life and ministry of the churches? Here are four suggestions:

(1) Local churches must have full responsibility for who serves them as their ministers. The power of the denomination to impose a non-evangelical ministry on a church against its will is unacceptable. Likewise the power to refuse to allow an evangelical ministry approved by the congregation is an abuse of denominational power.

If the denomination could be trusted to use such power to ensure the orthodoxy and good standing of ministers, it would be appropriate for the churches to delegate such power to the denomination. However, where the denomination can no longer be trusted to do that, then it has no right to hold onto that power.

There will be a down side to this. If the power to control ministry is taken from the denomination, it will not be able to prevent apostate congregations seeking heretical or immoral ministers. If it cannot really be trusted to do that anyway, then the power is in the wrong hands.

(2) Episcopal ordination must cease to be required for full gospel ministry in the local church.

This is a corollary to the first point. Episcopal ordination is the chief structural instrument of the Anglican denomination to control ministry. It was intended to be a form of recognition and authorisation of appropriate persons, properly prepared to be "shepherds of God's flock that is under your care, serving as overseers" (1Pet 5:2). The Ordinal of 1662 is a superb expression of this function. However, once episcopal ordination ceases to serve this purpose, but instead authorises inappropriate persons and refuses to authorise appropriate persons, then it cannot continue to be the *sine qua non* of ministry in our churches.

(3) The denomination must not control who is trained for gospel ministry in our churches.

The denomination is often in control of funds which support the training of ministers. This is a further instrument of control. While it is used for the purpose of training faithful gospel ministers, the funds are being used responsibly. However if, either through shortage of funds or changed understandings of Christian ministry, able evangelicals are refused training, other funds and training paths should be found.

(4) Steps must be taken to put church property under the control of the local congregation.

Today's denominations generally control vast amounts of land and property. These have been inherited from the past. Whatever the particulars of the law, these inheritances are trusts. Once again denominational ownership of church property is an instrument of control which may be exercised responsibly for the advance of the gospel, or may be used to obstruct and prevent evangelical ministry. When the latter position is reached, faithful congregations have a moral right to control the property entrusted from the past for gospel ministry.

While such changes call for careful wisdom, they are too urgent for procrastination. One of the rules of thumb for changes in a denomination that has lost a clear gospel commitment should be: if a proposal increases the power of the centre, oppose it; if it frees the life of the local congregation, support it. These matters cannot wait for twenty years. In ten years it will probably be too late.

Denominational loyalty

A denomination, once it has developed, appears typically to demand the loyalty of the individual churches and their members to the association itself. The denomination very easily loses sight of its proper role of encouraging faithfulness to Christ and to all who belong to him. Instead of being a means to this end, the denomination becomes an end in itself.

Loyalty is not a Christian virtue. Indeed it can be sinful. We have the expression "blind loyalty." The Christian virtue is faithfulness, and faithfulness is exercised towards persons, not institutions. Faithfulness to Christ is our first duty, as he has been faithful to us. Faithfulness to our brothers and sisters into whose company God has drawn us is a second. Faithfulness to brothers and sisters beyond our circles is a third.

Loyalty to a denomination is often expected in exclusive terms. Relations with believers of the same denomination is seen to take precedence over relations with other believers. It may be regarded as disloyal (or improper in some other way) when a person moves to a different town if he/she joins a church of a different denomination. Participating in activities or projects with other churches is frowned on, or at least should take second place to participation with one's own denomination. All of this is an improper expression of denominationalism.

The scandal of denominationalism (which is not inherent in the concept, neither is it necessary in practice) is the creation of *barriers* to fellowship with those who do not belong to that denomination, based on the traditions of men. When the denomination has gained some control over the life of its member churches, then barriers to fellowship can be imposed within the congregation. Do I have to be loyal to "Anglicanism" before I am accepted in this local church?

Then things are upside down. The denomination exists to foster the Christian fellowship of member churches, not to create barriers to fellowship with other churches!

Are you a "loyal" member of the Church of England? I sincerely hope not!

Denominational distinctiveness

It is only natural that an association of churches that has a history will develop some distinctive expressions of their relationship, or distinctive ways of doing things which they share.

There would appear to be no great problem with this in principle, until these distinctives become regarded as essentials. Once the distinctives of your denomination become part of your religion, your denomination has become a sect. Once the distinctives (of dress, liturgy, polity, or other practice) become hindrances to relating to believers who do not share these distinctives, then the distinctives must be challenged.

The problem appears to be that the denomination becomes concerned for its own identity. How much has been written about the Anglican identity crisis!? If only that identity crisis had arisen because members of this association did not care about being different from their brothers and sisters outside that denomination! If only it was because Anglicans had learnt to sit loose to their sub-culture, and cared only about those things they share with "all those everywhere who call on the name of our Lord Jesus Christ." Then we could say, who cares about Anglican identity? It does not matter! Alas, I fear that the reasons for the crisis are rather different. However, should not evangelicals at least be genuinely unconcerned about their Anglican identity, for the reasons I have mentioned? It does not matter at all that a denomination maintain its distinctiveness. That is Babylonian.

It is not to be wondered at, then, if evangelicals tend to take the lead in dispensing with denominational distinctives that have no basis in God's word, and have lost any usefulness in expressing the spiritual unity and fellowship between churches. I would include here distinctive titles, distinctive clothing and commitment to distinctive Anglican polity. Certainly changes in these areas may, depending on circumstances, require patience and wisdom. There may be circumstances where change is not possible or desirable. But we ought not to be among those who resist changes *because of Anglican identity*. Uniformity of distinctive practices between churches of a denomination is of no spiritual value. It establishes a false unity, which all to easily substitutes for the unity of the Spirit, and has done so. It is Babylonian unity.

4. The unity of the Spirit is both smaller and larger than the denomination

Now I would like to draw out some implications of the understanding of unity, church and denomination that we have been considering.

Evangelicals claim to be gospel people. We must not allow this claim to be the basis for arrogance. Then it would be a claim falsely made. For the gospel humbles all whom it touches. We are miserable sinners, saved by the extraordinary grace of our God.

Humility, however, demands our submission to the word of God and our recognition that biblical gospel Christianity is authentic Christianity. We are far from perfect either in our confession or our obedience. But if evangelicals have become one sub-group in our various denominations, then we have to insist that our claim is that it is only believing the gospel of Jesus Christ found in Holy Scripture, only trusting in the Jesus of that gospel, that makes a man or a woman a member of the church of God.

We must not confuse the unity of the Spirit with the unity of the denomination. Let me speak from my own situation. The denomination with which I am associated is known as the Anglican Church of Australia. What is the Anglican Church of Australia in fact (as distinct from what it claims to be)? What do the members of the Anglican Church of Australia actually have in common? The honest answer is: real estate and money. The Anglican Church of Australia has (not inappropriately) been described as a religious real estate company and long service leave provider. In addition, the association called the Anglican Church of Australia provides interesting forums for discussions of all kinds of issues. It makes rules as to what you can and cannot do on property owned by the association. But it is fanciful in the extreme to think that it is a fellowship of persons or churches who agree on anything to do with the gospel!

At the same time, the Anglican Church of Australia does provide a link between some of its members who are converted people, and some Bible believing churches. The real estate company can therefore provide a mechanism for such churches to meet with each other, work together and help and be helped. The unity of the Spirit can be experienced and expressed, even fostered, within these Anglican structures. But the structures are not themselves an expression of anything of the kind. Perhaps they once were: the Constitution agreed to in 1961 certainly makes grander claims for the association than I am here recognising.

How should evangelical Christians in such denominations think about their Christian relationships?

The unity of the Spirit is unity in the gospel

First, we must be people whose focus is on the gospel, its true understanding, and its faithful proclamation in the power of the Spirit. The unity that matters to us, and the only unity that matters, must be the unity created by God himself through this gospel, unity *in* this gospel. Only unity in this gospel is the unity of which the gospel speaks.

The very great (perhaps the greatest) folly of Anglicanism is to take pride in the slogan "unity in diversity," when what is meant is unity in Anglican distinctives that do not matter and diversity in what is believed. There is unity where there should be diversity and diversity where there should be unity!

The unity that matters to us is agreement in the gospel: one faith, one hope, one calling. Therefore we will not neglect the study of the gospel, the discussion of the gospel, the working together through differences that arise. We will not take the gospel for granted, as though we all know it so well. We will contend for the gospel. It will matter to us when it is denied, compromised or ignored. We will care about the disagreements that arise among us, and work hard at coming to one mind. For example, we will not be content to pretend that the differences between evangelicals and charismatics do not matter. The serious study and exposition of the Scriptures will be at the centre of our activities.

We will contend for the gospel in the forums of our denomination, whether or not they are interested, and whether or not we "have the numbers." We will contend for the proclamation of the gospel in this land, and throughout the world. We want to discern where denominational structures or rules can help the progress of the gospel, and recognise that the association has no right to hinder the gospel. And when it does we oppose it, or bypass it, or get around it.

We will be more concerned for the prospering of believing churches than for the prospering of the denomination. It is in the churches and from the churches (not from the real estate company) that we expect the gospel to grow.

In our denominational activities we must resist the temptation to be men pleasers. All too frequently evangelicals who get involved in the denominational structures are tempted to dissociate themselves from other evangelicals who are less committed to the denomination (not "Anglican" enough). That is unfaithfulness.

Our unity with those who agree in the gospel is too important for that game to be played.

The unity of the Spirit divides the denomination

Second: we must expect that the unity of the Spirit will divide the denomination.

If we are committed to unity and avoiding division, we will not be faithful to the gospel. It will never be the "right time" to push gospel issues hard. There will always be reasons to put off action.

When the Sydney synod agreed to a proposal to authorise lay administration of the Lord's Supper, the cry from many evangelicals was: "Not now! Not while we are trying to get a hearing in the homosexual debate. Not while we are trying to get evangelical clergy into other dioceses. Not while there is a chance of having more evangelical bishops appointed round the place. Not while we are negotiating to get more Anglican candidates to study at Moore College. It's a good idea, but it is not the right time."

In that case it never will be the right time. We need to learn and accept that the gospel and gospel mindedness *will divide* denominations.

I loathe conflict more than I am able to tell you. And may God deliver us from people who relish a fight. But we cannot be gospel people if we will not accept that it is good for the differences to come to the surface: for the unity of the Spirit to take absolute priority over the unity of the denomination. I do not *want* the Anglican Church of Australia to be united (unless, of course, it comes to be united in the gospel). When I am involved in a denominational study group, I want the report to make clear *how much we disagree*, not to come up with a set of words that hides our disagreements and portrays an illusion of unity. Denominational unity is Babylonian unity, and typically an *alternative*, a *rival*, to the unity of the Spirit. If you are for one, I do believe that you will be against the other. I want us to develop the mindset that understands that if a proposal will be divisive, that is *prima face* evidence that it is a good idea, and probably that now is the time to do it! Because I like a fight? No! Because the unity of the Spirit does divide.

The unity of the Spirit demands trans-denominational fellowship

Evangelicals must ensure that we are responsive to the Spirit of God who draws us in love towards "all those everywhere who call on the name of our Lord Jesus Christ" (1Cor 1:2).

If we are responsive to the Holy Spirit, we will not only be drawn to fellowship with fellow Anglicans. If we are, it would seem that we are responding to something other than the Spirit of God, who knows no such limitations.

I have been suggesting that we ought to take up opportunities given by our denominational association for believing churches to relate to other faithful churches. However, it is particularly important, and especially if our denominational structure happens to be dominant (as in the Church of England and the Anglican Church in Sydney), that we express our unity with gospel people and churches across recognised denominational boundaries.

I know that Reform has looked at this question. I have seen some most interesting proposals. Evangelicals working together, fellowshipping across denominational limits for the sake of gospel churches and gospel proclamation will, at some point, encounter denominational opposition. That may well be an indication that we are on the right track.

To conclude: Let us value denominations for what they are, but appreciate clearly what they are not. It is ever so important that evangelicals repudiate the idea that our Christian identity is associated with our denominational label. The folly of denominational loyalty expresses walking by sight, not by faith. Our agenda with respect to our denomination must be the good of churches and the spread of the gospel. When the denomination loses its usefulness for those ends, it has lost its usefulness for anything, and there is no point at all in sticking with it.

Conclusion:
The Unity that Helps and The Unity that Hinders

The importance of the subject that has occupied us in these pages cannot be overstated. We began with the prayer of Jesus "that all of them may be one, Father, just as you are in me and I am in you" (John 17:21). *That* unity is the beginning of God's ultimate purpose for all things:

> *... to be put into effect when the times will have reached their fulfilment—to bring all things in heaven and on earth under one head, even Christ.* (Eph 1:10)

However our argument has been that this unity must be distinguished from other kinds of "unity." The unity for which Jesus prayed was established by his death and is experienced by those who are called by the gospel, to whom the word of Christ crucified is "the power of God and the wisdom of God" (1Cor 1:24). This unity is expressed in agreement as to the truth of the gospel (see 1Cor 1:10 and 15:1-11) and behaviour towards one another that is worthy of the calling by which we were called (Eph 4:1-2).

To guard this unity calls for the wisdom to discern the difference between two kinds of unity, two kinds of diversity and two kinds of division.

Two kinds of unity

The unity that matters to us supremely must be the unity of the new humanity God has created by the death of his Son, and that he is calling into being by the one true gospel. This gospel unity is unity *in* the gospel, unity in the Christ of the gospel, unity in the Father and the Son by the Spirit. It is the unity of the body of Christ, the one church "built on the foundation of the apostles and prophets, with Christ Jesus himself as the chief cornerstone" (Eph 2:20).

The other unity is what humans create in their pride, arrogance and defiance of God. It is worse than worthless. It is unity in Babylon, and will fall under God's judgment. The unity of a denomination that does not agree in the truth of God's Word is this kind of unity. To guard or strive to maintain this kind of unity is to set oneself *against* the unity of the Spirit. Today the confused belief that this kind of unity, in its denominational expression, is pleasing to God is a major hindrance to the work of the gospel.

Two kinds of diversity

We have noted that unity is not the same thing as equivalence or sameness. The expression "unity in diversity" is valid.

However, what makes all the difference in the world is which kind of unity, and therefore what kind of diversity? Being united in the human traditions and customs of Anglicanism with diversity in faith is Babylonian. Being united in the one gospel with diversity of church order and other similar things is surely the unity of which the gospel speaks, the unity God has created.

Evangelicals must be committed to the second kind of diversity, but disown the first.

Two kinds of division

Finally there are two kinds of division that must be carefully distinguished.

There is division caused by the gospel between those to whom the word of the cross is foolishness and those to whom it is the power of God. This division will be found in the world, in our denominations and in local congregations. It is never pleasant. It is the consequence of the sin of unbelief. However it is necessary (1Cor 11:19) and evangelicals must not be afraid to accept or even cause this kind of division.

There is also division based on human "boasting" which is a denial of the gospel. Division between people based on and caused by human preferences, ambitions, selfcentredness and the like have no place in Christ's church. Evangelicals must oppose and where necessary repent of this kind of division.

John Woodhouse lectured at Moore College, Sydney, for 20 years in Old Testament before becoming rector at St Ives parish church in the diocese of Sydney. He has, however, recently been appointed Principal of Moore College. He is married to Moya and has four adult children

This booklet is published by Reform and is available from the Reform office. The cost is £2.00 including postage. The text is also available on our web site - www.reform.org.uk

Further information about Reform can be obtained from:
The Reform office
PO Box 1183
Sheffield
S10 3YA
Tel: 0114 230 9256